the Divine Feline

Also by Belinda Alexandra

White Gardenia

Wild Lavender

Silver Wattle

Tuscan Rose

Golden Earrings

Sapphire Skies

Southern Ruby

The Invitation

The Mystery Woman

the Divine Feline

A CHIC CAT LADY'S GUIDE TO WOMAN'S BEST FRIEND

BELINDA ALEXANDRA

murdoch books
Sydney | London

Published in 2020 by Murdoch Books, an imprint of Allen & Unwin

Murdoch Books Australia
83 Alexander Street,
Crows Nest NSW 2065
Phone: +61 (0)2 8425 0100
murdochbooks.com.au
info@murdochbooks.com.au

Murdoch Books UK
Ormond House, 26–27 Boswell Street,
London WC1N 3JZ
Phone: +44 (0) 20 8785 5995
murdochbooks.co.uk
info@murdochbooks.co.uk

Publisher: Kelly Doust
Editorial Manager: Julie Mazur Tribe
Design Manager and Designer: Madeleine Kane
Editor: Melody Lord
Illustrator: Neryl Walker / The Jacky Winter Group
Production Director: Lou Playfair
Cover design by Madeleine Kane

ISBN 978 1 76052 575 0 Australia
ISBN 978 1 91163 286 3 UK

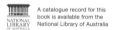

A catalogue record for this
book is available from the
National Library of Australia

A catalogue record for this book is available from the National Library of Australia
A catalogue record for this book is available from the British Library

Printed by Hang Tai Printing Company Limited, China

DISCLAIMER: The content presented in this book is meant for inspiration and informational purposes only. The purchaser of this book understands that the author is not a veterinary professional, and the information contained within this book is not intended to replace professional advice. The author and publisher claim no responsibility to any person, animal or entity for any liability, loss or damage caused or alleged to be caused directly or indirectly as a result of the use, application or interpretation of the material in this book.

10 9 8 7 6 5 4 3 2 1

MIX
Paper from
responsible sources
FSC® C023121

To all the cats I have ever loved

Contents

Introduction

Throughout history women have had a special relationship with cats: from the ancient Egyptian priestesses in the temples of the goddess Isis, to witches of the Middle Ages and career women of today. This makes sense, as women and cats share many traits: beauty and elegance; sensitivity; affectionate natures; a knack for nurturing; and a love of the luxurious. Cats also embody the feminine dark side, with a tendency to neuroses and fear of change. Then there are those qualities that cats possess that women long to emulate. A cat will fight fiercely to protect itself; never says 'yes' when it means 'no'; and isn't afraid to claim the best seat in the house for itself. Cats are loyal to those who love them, but couldn't give a toss what people think of them. They don't suffer self-esteem issues

or worry if they are overweight. In addition, they exude an air of mystery in that slinky walk . . . oh, to be a cat!

Yet society has often driven a wedge between women and their cats, both physically and emotionally. In history, they were persecuted together during the witch-hunts, and even in modern times the lore of the 'crazy cat lady' persists. The 'cat lady' is thought of as a hermit and a hoarder. Shunned by society, she dies alone. Her body isn't discovered for weeks and when it is, she has been half-consumed by her ravenous cats. The story is a subtle warning to women who want to remain single, independent and childless: better get a husband and family or this could be you! (It's interesting that there is no equivalent of the 'crazy cat lady' for men.)

In this book you will find none of that. It is an unashamed celebration of the spiritual bond of feline and feminine that has been handed down to us from ancient times. I will describe the history of the relationship of women and cats through the ages and share the journey of my own life with cats, relating how they have influenced my writing. I'll also show you how to revive the sacred bond of the witch and her familiar (an animal that assists a wise woman to travel from the physical to the spiritual realm) by suggesting ways you can create a magical connection with your cat (or cats, as the situation may be).

As a lover of history, I'll share some endearing stories of famous people and their passion for cats, and as an amateur cat behaviourist I'll give you some insight into why cats do the things they do. I'll also provide information on how to understand the ways your cat communicates with you, suggest home remedies for simple ailments, and ponder with you on the question of whether it is possible to train a cat or not—they have certainly trained us! As a lover of all animals, and especially wildlife, I'll propose ways to both enjoy your cat and be mindful of all the other lives around you too. I'll also describe some ways to create a stimulating environment for indoor cats to take care of their psychological and physical needs.

But most of all this is a book about joy. Quite often women who love cats are made to feel guilty about it. We are almost compelled to describe ourselves as 'crazy cat ladies' by way of apology for our passion. There is a difference between a cat hoarder, who keeps herself and her animals in terrible conditions due to a tragic mental health issue or other trauma, and an everyday woman who happens to like cats and maybe even has several. You'll notice that I've taken the 'crazy' out of the subtitle of this book. I'm all for joshing and not taking ourselves too seriously, but you'll see when you read the history of women and cats that the belittling of the relationship has some dark undertones.

Apart from that, I am also a huge proponent of joy! It is an emotional state that adds zing to our lives, makes us better and more loving people, and gives us purpose. The best way to find joy is to fully and unapologetically indulge yourself in things that make you feel good. It is my hope that by understanding the divine bond between women and their cats you will be able to see the relationship you have with your cat in a new and magical light.

So make yourself a cup of tea (or coffee, hot chocolate, Champagne or whatever you fancy), settle down with your feline companion and delve into the world of *The Divine Feline*.

Enjoy!

Belinda Alexandra

Dear Pebbles,

I've always hated using the pronoun 'it' when talking about animals: he or she is preferable, but it can be messy and slightly confusing when writing about cats in general. Although I don't personally have a problem with the word 'pet' (the lady at the local fruit shop calls me 'pet' in the most affectionate manner), I appreciate that this can be considered belittling to our feline companions. What labels and pronouns would you recommend for this book?
Belinda

Dear Belinda,

The art of being correct is as delicate an operation as traversing the narrowest of fences, pretending to be adorably fast asleep when you are in someone else's favourite chair or sneaking titbits from the dinner table and then appearing innocent when somebody notices that there are no prawns in the Shrimp Fra Diavolo. That is because what is 'correct and appropriate' is like beauty: it exists in the eye of the beholder.

Let me share a little secret with you. We cats exist in a world of feelings, smells and sounds. Words are of little importance to us. How else could we put up with undignified names like Darth Kitty,

6

Meatloaf or King Fluffy Butt if we didn't feel the genuine love of those misguided beings who named us? You could say, 'You little devil incarnate, you hairy gremlin, you lumpatious little lump,' and we would lap it up as long as you said it in a soothing, sweet purring tone. And as for smells, don't even get me started . . .

Now, human beings are a different matter. No creature on earth is as easy to offend as a human, especially those humans who like to be offended on behalf of others. As your book will be read chiefly by your own kind, I suggest that you use the word 'companion' rather than 'pet' where appropriate. The term 'owner' will most likely cause confusion. Who is it exactly that is owned? The human or the cat? Those people fortunate enough to have one of us felines in their lives will understand that they are the ones who are 'owned', not us. Many people prefer to see themselves as 'guardians'—though it causes me to chuckle to think that any cat needs to be 'guarded'—which evokes a sense of the honour and privilege those humans hold in devoting their lives to a feline's every whim and need.

Perhaps the best thing you can do for your readers is to assure them that all conventions of language in *The Divine Feline* are used with the spirit in which the book is written: with deep love and reverence for the special bond between women and cats.

As we cats would say: 'Mrrh! Prrh! Meow! Meow! Meeeow!' (The meaning of a thing always depends on its context.)

Pebbles

1
Cat history

Where the kitty cat originated

While there has been some contention over the years, it is largely now agreed that the ancestor of the domestic cat is the African wildcat, *Felis silvestris lybica*. This cat still roams in northern Africa and the Middle East and it is well adapted to life in the desert. Its tawny fur and striped markings are the perfect camouflage against the sand and rocky outcrops. It resembles a large, elongated mackerel tabby.

What is most fascinating is that although the African wildcat has been around for five million years there is little difference between it and the domestic cat in terms of genetics and appearance. The domestic cat is slightly smaller than its African ancestor, gives birth to more litters a year and has a greater variety of coat colours. But all domestic cat breeds share this common ancestor. If you have ever suspected that, despite the highly privileged lifestyle you provide for your cat, there is something a little untamed about your furry friend, you are right.*

The love story between cats and humans began about 4000 BC when nomadic tribes settled along the Nile valley in Egypt and planted crops. Egypt became an agrarian society that relied on grain and the ability to store it in times of famine. Mice and rats can destroy a grain store in a matter of days and, while local snakes such as the deadly asp helped to keep the population of vermin under control, they weren't desirable to have around the house. Wildcats were likely attracted to the granaries by the steady supply of mice and rats, and farmers were more than pleased to have them around. They offered the cats tasty morsels of food and milk to drink to encourage them to stay. Cats always know when they are onto a good thing and a mutually beneficial relationship developed; possibly the tamer kittens born from these cats became used to human company and, preferring the shelter and luxuries offered to them over life in the wild, they stayed put.

Unlike other domesticated animals such as dogs, sheep and cows, cats were not bred for certain tasks. They were perfect

---

* *The Latin name for a domestic cat is* Felis catus. *You can use this term to impress your friends. For example: 'I have to go home now and feed my* Felis catus.'

as they were for rodent catching and as animal companions. As a result their appearance and behaviour are little changed.

In other words, cats chose us as much as we chose them. In fact, some go so far as to suggest that cats domesticated themselves. This could be the reason that cats have always maintained that intriguing air of self-possession and independence. They have never been our slaves or servants. We have never been their masters. We got cute companions who kept rodents away from our food supplies. In exchange, cats received treats, shelter, affection, adoration and eventually the status of gods.

Do you understand now why your cat might be just a touch haughty?

The original cat lovers

The alliance between cats and humans may have begun even earlier than predynastic Egypt. An African wildcat and a human skeleton have been uncovered in a Neolithic gravesite in Cyprus. The fact that the grave of the cat had been deliberately dug and that it had been buried in close proximity to the human suggests that the two were connected in some way. But the most significant and large-scale relationship of cats and humans formed in Egypt. Mice and rats not only destroyed the grain supplies, they brought diseases with them. The larger rats sometimes attacked infants and the elderly. Cats kept rodent populations under control, and they also disposed of dangerous snakes and scorpions with aplomb. Those households with a family cat or two prospered and also seemed to suffer less misfortune. As a result, cats became associated with good luck.

Any cat lover knows that when you invite a cat into your home you will eventually lose your heart to it. This seems to have been the case with Crown Prince Thutmose of the Eighteenth Dynasty (brother of Akhenaten), who had his pet she-cat mummified after her death and gave her a ceremonial burial. Thousands of cat mummies have been unearthed in Egypt. While some might have been temple cats, archaeologists believe many of them were companion cats of loving guardians who wished to assure them of an afterlife. Herodotus, the Greek historian, observed that in Egypt when a house caught fire it was only the cats that mattered, and when the family cat died the household members would shave their eyebrows and go into mourning.

With this sort of reverence for felines, it was only a matter of time before cats rose to the status of gods. The ancient Egyptians did not make a distinction between humans and other animals. Their religion was animism: the belief that all living and non-living things contained a spirit and reflected some aspect of the greater divinity. Therefore every person was able to make contact with the Divine directly themselves or through these beings. It was only later that the concept of almighty gods who needed the pharaohs and priests to act as intermediaries developed. It seemed that cats were able to bridge both forms of worship. With their dual natures—loving

and affectionate on one hand, fierce hunters and fighters on the other—cats were the animals most comparable to the gods, who could raise a pharaoh with one hand and then smite him with the other. The sun god Ra, the most powerful deity of all, was believed to take on the form of a cat each night and fight his great enemy, the snake-demon Apep. This meant that the sun could rise the next day.

Later, during the time of the Twenty-second Dynasty (945–715 BC), cats became associated with the revered Egyptian goddess Bastet, who had a magnificent temple in the city of Bubastis. Bastet originally started out as a lion-headed woman (the lion being closely associated with royalty), but in later periods her iconography changed to that of a cat. Archaeologists have uncovered thousands of small bronze statuettes of Bastet, suggesting that she was possibly the most popular goddess for households: a people's goddess, if you like. Although held sacred by both sexes, cats were most closely associated with women, especially in regard to fertility. Cats were noisy and ardent copulators, able to produce three litters a year. They were also elegant and clean animals that liked to groom themselves. Bastet was linked with sensual pleasures including perfume as well as being viewed as a practical protector.

Because cats were sacred, harming one was considered a crime. If a person came across a deceased cat, they would be sure to let everyone know that they had not been responsible for its death. Diodorus Siculus, another Greek historian, reported that even when Egypt was part of the Roman Empire an angry crowd murdered a Roman soldier who had accidentally killed a cat. Legend states that during the battle of Pelusium in 525 BC the attacking Persians had their front-rank soldiers carry cats and other sacred animals, knowing the Egyptians would be reluctant to shoot their arrows in case they hurt one of them.

Smuggling cats out of Egypt was forbidden, but it was hard to resist such a prized animal. If a foreign trader managed to do it, the army was sent to retrieve the cat or emissaries dispatched to diplomatically argue for its return.

To be labelled a 'crazy cat lady' has become something of a put-down. But I'm comforted by the fact that the original cat crazies were possibly the most advanced people on planet Earth at the time. The same civilisation that brought us paper, libraries and advances in mathematics, science and medicine had an obsession with felines that was probably equivalent to, if not greater than, the popularity that cats enjoy on the internet today.

....

It is easy to understand why the rabble dislike cats.
A cat is beautiful; it suggests ideas of luxury,
cleanliness, voluptuous pleasures.
Charles Baudelaire (French poet, 1821–1867)

Dear Pebbles,

My cat, Merlin, is destroying my love life. Whenever my boyfriend comes over to stay, Merlin pees on his clothes or on his side of the bed. What should I do?

Desperate

Dear Desperate,

The answer to this question is rather obvious to me. If Merlin doesn't like your boyfriend, get a new boyfriend! We cats sniff out a rat long before you do! But seriously, look at this from Merlin's point of view. How many nights has he sat faithfully by your side as you cried your heart out over some cad who was never good enough for you anyway? Now you are turning up with this new person who smells strange and, even worse, is getting those special smiles from you that used to be reserved for Merlin alone. And God forbid if you are shutting Merlin out of your bedroom when your boyfriend comes over! Merlin is simply reacting as any self-respecting feline would: like an insanely jealous lover! If this gentleman is really meant for you then he will go to as much trouble to win over Merlin as he does to win you over. This could include:

- ♥ Lightly misting his shoes and clothing with a synthetic cat pheromone product before he enters your home. This will make Merlin feel more comfortable with sharing his territory with this interloper.
- ♥ Arriving with a yummy treat for Merlin as well as flowers for you. Merlin will associate the arrival of your boyfriend with something positive, even if it really isn't.
- ♥ The three of you playing Merlin's favourite game together. A small toy on the end of a string is nearly always a winner.
- ♥ Making sure your boyfriend speaks softly and respectfully to Merlin and never whistles at him like a dog or tells him to 'scat'!

I'd also recommend that you allow Merlin to continue to share the bed with you along with your boyfriend, as 'cats' that sleep together bond together. If that's not possible then give Merlin the dignity of a far superior bed outside your room (perhaps one that is heated in winter and smells deliciously of catnip, with a 'turn-down' service that includes a cat treat).

Mind you, if you really want to win over Merlin, you should let him continue to sleep with you in your bed while your boyfriend gets the couch. Just saying!

Pebbles

The cat goes abroad

Although it was illegal to take a cat out of Egypt, some foreign sailors managed to do it—not only wanting the cats as symbols of good luck for dangerous voyages, but also to control the vermin populations on their ships. Cats may not like rough seas, but they do like fish and mice and maybe even cuddling up to a lonely sailor. A symbiotic relationship developed between felines and seafarers and to have a cat on board became the talisman of a safe voyage.

The Greeks were important traders with Egypt and it wasn't long before depictions of domestic cats began to appear on pots, artwork and coins in Greece as well as its colonies in Italy, France, Spain and the Balkans. While there is some conjecture about whether there had already been some domestication of wildcats native to Asia, it appears that cats from Egypt soon appeared after the opening of trade routes to India, China and Japan. Having arrived, cats quickly became popular in Asia because they kept rats away from the valuable silk cocoons. Oriental breeds of cats such as the Siamese and Burmese still share the DNA of the African wildcat.

The Romans helped to further spread the cat throughout their empire, including Britain. The Roman army employed felines to protect their military and food stores from vermin. Soldiers could not go into battle only to discover too late that their weaponry—manufactured using leather and sinew—had been gnawed at by rats. Again, cats became associated with good luck, but this time in battle.

Cats were not the only Egyptian export. Religion travelled from that ancient land all over Europe, including the cult of the goddess Isis. This goddess of fertility, childbirth, marriage and children had become entwined with Bastet during the Hellenistic period. Isis became a popular goddess throughout the Roman Empire and had more temples and shrines dedicated to her than any other deity. She was seen as the embodiment of all the gods and goddesses of the world, so no matter what religion you followed, you were worshipping some aspect of her.

Isis was the goddess of the night and the moon, and black was the colour of her robe. Black was considered a magical colour by the Egyptians. It was not viewed as symbolic of evil: it was simply the colour of the night. Isis was also believed to have the ability to transform herself into a cat. This may be one of the reasons a black cat was to become associated with her and with pagan worshippers in general.

Isis later merged with the goddess Artemis in Greece, and the goddess Diana in Rome. She was also associated with the Norse goddess Freya, who was believed to ride in a chariot pulled by two black cats.

Women had important leadership roles in the worship of Isis and were held in high regard in these times. They had rights that women for centuries after could only dream of, and would have to fight tooth and claw to get back, including the right to choose their own marriage partners, to own their own property, and to be awarded half the marriage assets in cases of divorce.

Powerful women, an almighty Goddess supreme above all, the magic moon and black cats. What could possibly go wrong?

The dark age for cats

Next time somebody tries to tell you that cats are of no practical use, spend all day sunning themselves or sleeping, and have done nothing to advance humankind, you might remind them that without the cat's rodent-catching abilities, civilisation might have taken another direction entirely.

Initially the Roman imperial era was good for women, pagans and cats. The central government was tolerant of diversity of religious beliefs and left different regions to express their unique cultural traditions as long as they didn't commit monstrous crimes such as murder (including human sacrifice, which was common at the time) and rape. If citizens paid their taxes on time, they were mostly left alone.

In return, the government undertook various public works, including waste disposal and the supply of clean water, which led to good standards of health and hygiene as well as advances in medicine.

Cats were considered valuable, on par with other domestic animals such as chickens, sheep and goats. They were accounted for in divorce settlements as they were regarded as assets.

Cat wisdom

Xenia

'Remember you are a queen, so act like one! Stop tolerating fools and quit wasting your headbutts on those who don't appreciate them.'

✳ ✳ ✳

The rule was that if the family had one cat, it went to the husband. But if there were several cats, the husband would get one and the rest went to the wife.

Things took a nasty turn with the rise of Christianity or, more accurately, with the misappropriation of it, as there is nothing in the teachings of Jesus that would support the brutality and ignorance that was to follow. In the early days of Christianity, women held important roles in the church, which reflected the regard Jesus showed toward them.

Paganism was a minestrone soup of religions, incorporating old gods, new gods, local deities, nature spirits, magic, genii and philosophy into its spiritualism. Its followers believed that the Creator's spirit inhabited all things: people were sacred, trees were sacred, cats were sacred, and so on. It's interesting that modern-day study of DNA seems to support this view. Humans share DNA with other creatures and even plants. Cat-lovers may be interested to know we share about 90 per cent of our DNA with felines; not much less than we share with primates such as chimpanzees (96 per cent).* This view allowed for tolerance of individual beliefs. Christianity, on the other hand, was dogmatic: there was one true God and one true way. Conversion, therefore, was important and apostles such as Paul were zealous about it. The Roman emperor Constantine used this fanaticism to consolidate his power. His new capital, Constantinople, contained Christian churches alongside pagan temples. The emperors who followed continued to encourage or even fully embrace Christianity. In 380 AD Emperor Theodosius I made it the official state religion.

The type of Christianity that arose from the teachings of the apostle Paul was strictly patriarchal. Women were ousted from their positions in the church, while those in the countryside were loath to embrace a new religion that devalued both them and nature. Why should they stop worshipping their beloved goddesses Isis and Diana?

---

* *Even more startling, perhaps, is that over half of our genetic code is identical to that of a banana!*

In the repressive atmosphere created by the new interpretation of Christianity, the notion of honouring nature—or even studying scientific principles—was considered demonic. Controlling people by keeping them ignorant was the objective. The library at Alexandria was destroyed by monks. The human body—especially the female body—was regarded as inherently sinful, therefore bathing, which had been an important part of Roman culture, was discouraged.

It was a dark time for all humanity, but for women and cats, things were about to get worse.

Witch-hunts of the Middle Ages

The new Roman emperors used Christianity as a force of conquest and unification, and the old pagan religions were driven out. The goddesses Isis and Diana were demonised; their temples were plundered and destroyed and their followers massacred.

Many of the advancements made by the earlier Greeks and Romans in public health and medicine were now disregarded and humankind went rapidly backwards. Waste piled up in the streets and the rivers and wells were contaminated with sewage. People stopped washing themselves and their clothes and began living in filthy conditions, wrongly believing that slovenliness was pleasing to God.

Violence became the order of the day and the chaos was further exacerbated by the invasion of Europe by Germanic and other barbaric tribes who destroyed and devastated the

cities. Charlemagne, leader of the Franks—a Germanic tribe living in the area that is France today—conquered the Saxon territories, expanding into what was later to become Germany. He also gained control of northern Italy along with the city of Rome, and fought the Moors in Spain.

As Charlemagne supported the papacy, Pope Leo III made him the first Holy Roman Emperor in 800 AD. Charlemagne ordered the death penalty for anyone still practising paganism and allowed torture in the case of 'witchcraft'.

As Isis and Diana were associated with cats, this was bad news not only for women but for their feline companions. To destroy an old religion, anything venerated by it must be devalued and associated with evil. Possessing a cat was considered evidence of witchcraft, as witches were supposed to be able to transform themselves into cats by the light of the moon. In 1233 Pope Gregory IX issued the *Vox in Rama*, which denounced cats as evil and gave divine sanction for their extermination, especially black ones, and the killing of their owners. So many women and cats (along with other 'demonic' animals such as hedgehogs and frogs) were rounded up, tortured and burned or drowned that in some villages no woman or cat remained.

The mass hysteria about witches that was unleashed would gradually grow to its full height from 1450–1750 and would result in the death of tens of thousands of women and children, and an uncounted number of cats and other animals. The killings in Europe would not come to a complete end until the late eighteenth century. The targets of these attacks were often the midwives and healers in their villages, educated women, elderly women who kept cats for company, women who had refused the advances of vengeful men, and women whose relatives wanted their property so falsely accused them of demon worship.

Many Christian celebrations were marked with cat torture and deaths, including St John's Day and the first Sunday of Lent, when live cats were roasted over bonfires, their agonised cries supposedly warding off evil spirits. In Ypres, Belgium, cats were dropped from the belfry tower of the Cloth Hall into the town square.

Cat wisdom

Sabine

'Kittens are cute, but they don't know anything. Grace and poise come with maturity. Value your experience more than your youth. (And give a motherless kitten a lick and a helpful nudge when she needs it.)'

✳ ✳ ✳

The ignorance, cruelty, squalid living conditions and the death of so many cats became the perfect breeding ground for rat infestations and disease. It is no accident that the bubonic plague swept through Europe, killing millions. The disease is spread by fleas, their favourite vector being the rat. While cats alone could not have stopped outbreaks of the plague—better hygiene, cleaner streets and regular washing would have gone a long way to prevent it—the destruction and devaluation of an efficient form of rodent control certainly did not help.

Charles Dickens

ENGLISH WRITER AND SOCIAL CRITIC

(1812–1870)

When the Dickens family's cat gave birth to kittens, she moved them one by one from the kitchen into a corner of Charles's writing room. After several attempts to have the kittens removed to other parts of the house, Dickens gave up when the mother cat brought them all back again. He wrote with the kittens frolicking around him. Eventually the kittens were given to good homes, but Dickens kept one for himself: a white male cat who was deaf and was so devoted to the writer that he followed him everywhere. Dickens loved to tell the story of one evening, when he was reading with his cat beside him and the light of his candle went out. Absorbed in his book, Dickens simply relit the candle, but soon afterwards noticed it flickering again. He looked up to see his cat deliberately snuff it out with his paw. Dickens got the message. He put the book aside and gave the cat the attention he was seeking.

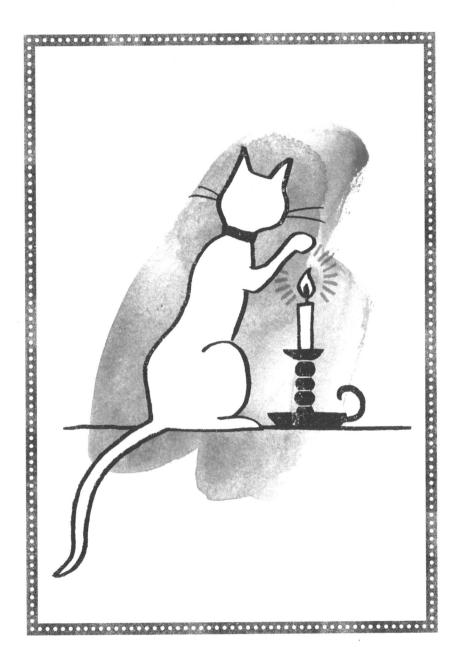

The cat in Islam

While the medieval church was intent on wiping out cats, the animal was highly appreciated in Islamic culture. Cats were viewed as clean, welcome to wander into mosques, and valued for their rodent-repelling skills, especially by scholars because they stopped mice from destroying entire libraries of books.

Far from being demonic, cats were regarded as spiritual helpers and a cat's purring was likened to prayer. God's presence, it is claimed, was manifested to the prophet Mohammed on occasion in the form of a white cat. In fact, it seems Mohammed was quite a cat lover, something he conveyed in his *Hadith* when he instructed that affection for cats is part of faith. He prohibited the persecution and killing of cats. His love of cats was shared by his friend, Abu Hurairah (whose name means: Father of a Kitten). According to one legend, Abu's cat saved Mohammed from a snakebite and in gratitude the prophet stroked the cat and blessed it with its righting reflex (a cat's ability to land on its feet). Some even say that the 'M' on a tabby's forehead is for the first letter of Mohammed's name!

There is a charming story that Mohammed's own cat, Muezza, once fell asleep on the sleeve of his prayer robe. When the prayer call sounded, rather than wake her, the prophet cut the sleeve off his robe and left her undisturbed.

Mohammed's kindness was shared by other Muslims, including the sultan Baibars who, when he died in 1277 AD, willed a perpetual sanctuary for cats in a garden in Cairo.

The cat makes a comeback

'Renaissance' and 'Enlightenment' are beautiful words with beautiful meanings. Renaissance refers to a revival and a renewal. Enlightenment means to develop a better understanding.

Both of these words refer to periods in history when humankind started to move forward again, after the brutality and darkness of the Middle Ages. These changes started at the top and took a while to trickle down to the masses, so it would still be some time before life improved for women and cats, but a crack of light was beginning to break.

The Renaissance

The Renaissance took place over the fourteenth to sixteenth centuries. It was a time of rediscovery of classical philosophy, literature and art. The role of the Roman Catholic church was questioned, and religion moved towards 'humanism'; a belief system that once again encouraged a personal relationship with the Divine.

Cats started appearing in Christian art, not as devils but as the embodiment of motherhood. In Federico Barocci's *The Madonna of the Cat*, Mary and the infant Jesus look on with benevolence as John the Baptist plays with a cat. There is some suggestion that Mary herself was seen as representative of the old earth mothers, Isis and Diana.

Leonardo da Vinci, perhaps the greatest genius humankind has yet produced, was not only ahead of his time in terms of aerodynamics, anatomy and mechanics, but also in his appreciation of the cat. His drawing *Cats, lions and a dragon* displays cats in a way that brings their charm and playfulness to life. He also likened the feline form to a masterpiece.

The Renaissance was a period of world exploration and it may be that domestic cats first reached the shores of America on the ships of Christopher Columbus.

The Enlightenment

The Enlightenment was an intellectual movement of the seventeenth and eighteenth centuries. It was an age when science blossomed and revolutions in the United States and France broke out. Good sanitation was once again viewed as important and education rather than ignorance was revered. The growing middle class gave rise to writers, scientists, philosophers and artists. The cat became a symbol, not of witchcraft, but of independence and cleanliness, and was adopted as a favoured animal companion by those who espoused the individual pursuit of happiness. Poets and philosophers such as Jeremy Bentham and Alexander Pope claimed that animals had a right to pursue happiness too, and should be protected against cruelty. There was an increased interest in the old religion of paganism and its appreciation of nature, of which the cat had previously been an important element.

Women, especially those in high society, were free to express their love for their feline companions. French harpist

Mademoiselle Dupuy credited her tomcat as her muse and made provision for him in her will with a townhouse in the city, an estate in the country, and a servant to wait on him for the rest of his years. Before the Revolution, women of the French court lavished their angora cats with attention. Like the Egyptians' cats before them, they were remembered with elaborate tombstones on their demise.

Of course poverty of the masses was still a major issue during the Enlightenment, as was the horror of slavery. Humankind still had a long way to go, but things were definitely on the way up for cats!

The cat victorious

The reign of Queen Victoria of the United Kingdom of Great Britain and Ireland, from 1837 to 1901, was an explosion of inventions, progress and reforms. The Industrial Revolution saw people flock from the countryside to live in cities. The catchwords of the age could have been 'advancement' and 'curiosity'.

Travelling was no longer only for explorers. The burgeoning wealth of the middle classes and the expansion of the railways, along with British colonialism, bred generations of intrepid tourists. Egypt, with all its magic and mysticism, was a popular destination and an enthusiasm for archaeology brought about a renewed interest in the goddess Bastet.

For those who could not travel, new museums, public aquariums and exhibitions brought the world to them. In fact,

Victorians loved the exotic so much that they brought it into their homes. Cabinets of curiosities became popular items in Victorian drawing rooms, and no parlour was complete without a rare orchid snatched by flower-hunters willing to risk venomous snakes, tigers and angry natives to bring treasures home.

While the upper classes were out hunting the big cats of Africa, India and Asia to near extinction, the middle-class Victorian family became obsessed with the miniature version that curled up on their laps as they read Jules Verne's *Around the World in 80 Days*. Cats reaffirmed their place with women, because what symbolised a tranquil, well-ordered home better than a cat sleeping peacefully by the fire? Cats, along with dogs, were now included in family portraits.

Anthropomorphic depictions of cats appeared, such as Beatrix Potter's Mrs Tabitha Twitchit, a shopkeeper and the mother of three scallywag kittens, Moppet, Mittens and Tom Kitten. The Victorians adored knick-knacks, and images of cute cats now appeared on all forms of home decor from teapots to clocks, inkwells, tapestry cushions and weathervanes.

It's no secret that Queen Victoria was a great animal lover. As well as her many beloved dogs, parrots, donkeys and ponies, she was partial to a fluffy white cat that she named White Heather. It was Queen Victoria who gave Royal status to the Society for the Prevention of Cruelty to Animals (RSPCA) and set the stage for many society women to take up the cause of homeless cats and dogs.

Winston Churchill

BRITISH PRIME MINISTER (1874–1965)

Winston Churchill was an animal lover with a soft
spot for cats. He nearly always had a feisty feline with
him at 10 Downing Street or at his private residences.
A grey cat named Nelson frequently attended formal
dinners and official meetings when Churchill was prime
minister. For his 88th birthday, Churchill was given a
marmalade cat; he named the cat Jock and wouldn't
eat dinner if his feline companion wasn't present.
Jock had a special place on the back seat of the car
whenever Churchill needed to travel. So attached
were the pair, that Churchill and his family requested
that after Churchill's death there should always be a
marmalade cat named Jock in residence at the family's
country estate, Chartwell. The National Trust has
honoured this request: since the original Jock passed
away, he has had a number of successors. Jock VI,
a rescue cat, is now in residence there.

The modern cat

There are three things to say concerning cats at the beginning of the twentieth century: armies, aviators and artists.

It is estimated that there were perhaps half a million cats in the Allied trenches during World War I, most of them recruited especially to kill rats. They were also used to detect gas; it would kill them faster than it would the soldiers—we can only speculate how many died. They continued to be employed as mousers on naval ships during conflicts. This was the case for World War II legend Oscar, who was rescued by the crew of the British destroyer HMS *Cossack* when they found him floating on a piece of wreckage after the sinking of the German battleship *Bismarck*. Black-and-white Oscar was soon to earn the nickname 'Unsinkable Sam' after he also survived the subsequent sinking of the *Cossack* by a submarine torpedo that resulted in the death of 159 of its crew. Unsinkable Sam's duties were transferred to the aircraft carrier HMS *Ark Royal*, which was subsequently torpedoed. He was discovered clinging to a floating plank and his condition was described by his rescuers as 'angry but quite unharmed'. Testing out his nine lives, no doubt, Unsinkable Sam was then put upon the HMS *Lightning*, which ultimately sank in 1943, although by then the cat had already been given land duties at the offices of the Governor of Gibraltar. Unsinkable Sam was later sent back to Britain, where he lived out the rest of his long life at a seaman's home in Belfast.

Cat wisdom

Scarlett

'Always know how to make yourself feel good: groom yourself; sit in the sunshine; run around the house in a kittenish burst of energy; or just watch the world go by for a while. Having a repertoire of feel-good activities that you incorporate into your day means you will keep yourself in a positive state of mind and life will sparkle!'

✳ ✳ ✳

Cats were not only considered good-luck charms by those who travelled on ships, but by aviators too. Felix the Cat was the most important cartoon icon of the silent-film era. He was mischievous, but ultimately charming and good hearted, always willing to help someone in need. A feisty and resourceful feline, he was loved by children and adults alike. It was Felix's image that many American World War II bomber and fighter pilots painted on their aircraft, symbolising deftness and the ability to conquer all.

The 'King of Aviators', American daredevil and flight instructor John Bevins Moisant, was the first pilot to take 'passengers' across the English Channel: his mechanic and his beloved cat, Mademoiselle Fifi. Moisant died in an air accident while making a preparatory flight for the 1910 Michelin Cup for the longest sustained flight of the year. It was one of the few occasions when Mademoiselle Fifi hadn't accompanied him in his plane; however, she did attend his funeral in full mourning dress.

Although Charles Lindbergh was known to take his cat, Patsy, with him on his pioneering flights, the welfare of felines was something he was always concerned about. Before his historic transatlantic flight in 1927, a mechanic handed him a stray kitten that had been found living in the hangar and suggested that he take it with him as a mascot. Lindbergh declined, believing the flight would be too cold and dangerous for such a young cat. He took a Felix the Cat doll instead.

While it was dogs, monkeys and mice that were the animals most often sent by the Soviet Union, the United States and other countries into outer space, the French did send a black-and-white cat, Félicette, aboard a rocket in 1963. She survived the flight but was euthanised later so scientists could examine her brain. The idea that innocent and terrified animals should be treated this way makes many of us shiver. Fans of my book *Sapphire Skies* will remember that the mysterious old lady's dog was named Laika, in honour of the street dog that was sent into space by the Soviet Union in 1957. Oleg Gazenko, one of the Soviet scientists responsible for the experiment, was later to express his regret. 'We shouldn't have done it . . . we did not learn enough from this mission to justify the death of the dog.'

It seems only natural that those who love beauty, form, elegance and mystery would succumb to a cat's charm. Some of the most famous artists of the twentieth century were obsessed with them: Picasso, Dalí, Kandinsky. Henri Matisse found comfort in his cats while he was bedridden in the last years of his life. Gustav Klimt loved cats and let them wander around his studio freely, as did Argentine surrealist painter Leonor Fini. Some of Fini's works can be identified by the stray cat hairs that stuck to the paint. Fini was a cat woman after my own heart. Not only was she known for her depictions of powerful independent women, often posed with cats, but she was also an animal activist. Although she had possibly fifty cats during her lifetime, every single one of them was dear to her and the loss of any one always caused her deep grief. But while they were living, they not only got to sleep in bed with her but also accompanied her on holidays, driven in their own car!

....

Of course, every cat is really the most beautiful woman in the room. That is part of their deadly fascination.
E.V. Lucas (English writer, 1868–1938)

Matthew Flinders

ENGLISH NAVIGATOR WHO IDENTIFIED
AUSTRALIA AS A CONTINENT (1774–1814)

Matthew Flinders' cat, Trim, is almost as famous as the man himself. The cat was born on board HMS *Reliance* as Flinders and his crew were sailing from the Cape of Good Hope to Botany Bay. The black-and-white kitten caught Flinders' eye when it toppled overboard but managed to swim back to the boat, scramble up a rope and get back onto the deck. Flinders admired the cat's determination. The two were to share many adventures on the high seas, including being shipwrecked on the Great Barrier Reef. Trim also kept Flinders company when the navigator was placed under house arrest in the French colony on Mauritius. When Trim did not return after one of his outdoor adventures, Flinders was heartbroken over the loss of his faithful friend. Flinders wrote *A Biographical Tribute to the Memory of Trim* and numerous statues in England and Australia pay tribute to the intrepid explorer—Trim, that is!

The cat today

The cat is once again enjoying status as a cultural icon. With the explosion of social-media sites such as Facebook, Instagram and YouTube, cats are far in the lead in terms of interest: way ahead of holiday selfies, wedding snaps and beauty-haul videos. Why? Research indicates that watching cats do all sorts of cat-like things—suddenly bursting out from under sofas, jumping in and out of boxes, waking their owners—makes us feel good. Interestingly, it's not elderly ladies in crocheted bedjackets who are leading this trend. It's the Millennials who can't get enough cat content!

Just as social media has launched human celebrities such as the Kardashians, Taylor Swift and Kanye West to dizzying heights, the cat world has produced its own superstars and petfluencers. Tardar Sauce, better known as Grumpy Cat, who sadly passed away in 2019, was a trailblazer. The feline dwarfism that gave her a permanently disgruntled air did not stop her living life to the fullest and launching a multimillion-dollar empire, including a soft toy and clothing line, as well as having her wax figure put on display at Madame Tussauds. The reigning Tom and Queen are Maru, who achieved a Guinness World Record in 2016 for having the most views for an animal on YouTube (more than 325 million views, although the record has since been surpassed), and Nala, a rescue cat, who has 4.2 million—and rising—Instagram followers. Other glittering stars include Lil Bub, Scarface, Hamilton the Hipster Cat,

Grumpy Cat

Streetcat Bob and, my favourite, Henrí, the existential cat, who recently retired to work on his opus, *The Old Cat and The Flea.*

Feline heroes

Cats are not only strutting their fashion ranges through social media; the internet can also be a platform to dispel the myth that cats are nothing more than loafers. When four-year-old Jeremy Triantafilo of California was saved from a vicious dog attack by the family cat, Tara, the video went viral. Masha, a longhair cat who lived in an apartment building in Russia, saved an abandoned baby from freezing to death by snuggling up to her and keeping her warm until the infant was found by residents. Australian yachtsman Grant McDonald owes his life to his first mate and cat, Major Tom, who alerted him that their boat was sinking. Add to that the cats that have turned their guardians away from suicide, warned them of impending dangers or roused them from diabetic seizures, and we can be assured that cats are not the idlers they are often made out to be.

With such an online presence, it's no surprise that there is now an international 'CatCon', where cat ladies and gentlemen from all over the world can gather to share their passion for all things feline. Since its inception in 2014, CatCon has swiftly turned into the world's largest cat lovers' convention. What I love most about the idea is that rescue cats of all ages and sizes are available at the convention for adoption into loving forever homes.

Cats are now the most popular warm-blooded animal companion in the United States, China, Russia, France, Germany, Brazil and Italy and are almost on par with dogs in Australia and the United Kingdom. With the uptake of apartment living in cities where single-dwelling habitation was once the norm, the increase in one-person households and the ageing population, the cat's popularity as a companion is set to grow even further.

While the cat's role as a rodent deterrent has been replaced by other methods of control, it has taken on a new duty in helping to stem the deadly epidemic that is sweeping modern civilisation: loneliness. Because loneliness is believed to be as incapacitating as any chronic disease and almost as bad for you as smoking fifteen cigarettes a day, Britain formed a Loneliness Strategy, overseen by the Minister for Loneliness, in 2018. Patting a purring cat is said to reduce stress and anxiety, and having a living creature to care for gives many people a reason to get up in the morning.

This was certainly proved to be true during the 2020 pandemic when people were asked to stay indoors and life as we all knew it turned upside down. Animal companions were a tremendous source of comfort to many people, especially those who were living alone, and pet-rescue adoptions were at an all-time high.

Cats and other animal companions are now regarded not so much as pets but as family members. As more cats than ever live indoors, their guardians have had the opportunity to observe and interact with them closely. This has led to an explosion of interest in cat behaviour. While cat products have lagged behind those manufactured for dogs, birds and fish for decades, there now is a wide range of accessories that is available to provide stimulating environments for cats: spectacular towers, interactive toys and bespoke scratching posts among them.

Thanks to the work started by the RSPCA in the nineteenth century, the number of animal charities and lobby groups has increased exponentially. Cruelty to animals is punishable by law in many countries (try burning women and their cats now!) and the subject of the legal rights of animals is a new area of discussion and debate.

This leads me back to the spiritual nature of our relationship with cats, which is something the ancient Egyptians understood. Now that we are no longer under the thumb of religions that put humankind at the apex of creation and teach that animals do not have souls, so we are free to treat them as we wish, many of us have turned to a modern spirituality akin to paganism. We believe all life is interconnected and we cannot do damage to one part without making the whole sick. Science increasingly supports this view.

As human beings we are always evolving, stumbling, making mistakes and ultimately improving. I have faith that despite all our shortcomings we are on a journey to our greatest potential. And as we make that journey, with all its sufferings and triumphs, our feline companions will be right alongside us, as they have always been: our fellow divine beings, our familiars, our inspiration.

More fascinating reading on the history of the cat

* *Classical Cats: The rise and fall of the sacred cat,* by Donald W. Engels (Routledge, 1999)
* *Famous Felines: Cats' lives in fact and fiction,* by David Alderton (Pen & Sword Books, 2009)
* *Revered and Reviled: A complete history of the domestic cat,* by Laura A. Vocelle (Great Cat Publications, 2016)
* *Sekhmet & Bastet: The feline powers of Egypt,* by Lesley Jackson (Avalonia, 2018)
* *The Cat in Ancient Egypt,* by Jaromir Malek (University of Pennsylvania Press, 1997)
* *When Cats Reigned Like Kings: On the trail of the sacred cats,* by Georgie Anne Geyer (Transaction Publishers, 2012)

Not quite out of the woods yet

Even though cats have come a long way since they were tortured and burned alongside their female guardians during the witch-hunts, today's cats still face—and present—some serious problems.

There is the issue of oversupply, and the lack of responsibility exercised by too many people, that results in staggering numbers of companion animals being euthanised in pounds and shelters and by other means each year. Many thousands of cats are left to live precarious lives on the streets of our cities. Desexing all companion animals and discouraging backyard breeding and impulse acquisition of companion animals (especially around Christmas) are some solutions to these problems.

Cats, along with other unfortunate animals, are still used in research laboratories where they are subjected to invasive, painful, stressful and nearly always fatal experiments. While all of us want cures for diseases that cause so much suffering in our human population, we also need to support scientists who are pushing for better alternatives to animal research. Hope is on the horizon with improved imaging and technology and also a greater interest in integrated medicine. While the number of animals used for experimentation has been dropping since the 1970s, more action and the development of superior alternative methods is needed in order to bring an end to the practice entirely.

Cats that roam outside the home can have devastating consequences for local wildlife. In fact, cats are classified as one of the world's 100 worst invasive species* by the International Union for the Conservation of Nature and are particularly destructive to the sensitive ecological systems found in Australia. Cat guardians have the ability to significantly diminish this impact by keeping cats inside, especially at night when their hunting instinct is strongest, or by providing garden enclosures where their cats can ⋯→

Interestingly, human beings do not consider themselves an 'invasive species', although we have dispersed ourselves to every continent as well as the ocean, the skies and even outer space, sending many species into extinction, destroying our environment and annihilating ancient cultures in the process. We overconsume and produce too much waste for our planet to sustain. Even more galling, perhaps, is that we put our genius to use building weapons of mass destruction that could blow the world to smithereens. While cats do have a significant impact on wildlife species, a fact that needs to be taken seriously, it's important that they don't become the sole scapegoats for the destruction of life on Earth. It's easy to blame cats, but harder to curb our own appetites.

enjoy the benefits of fresh air and sunshine without doing harm to wildlife. Getting both male and female companion cats desexed will also help reduce some of the problems caused by cats wandering further afield or trying to escape their homes, driven by the need to mate, and the spraying, fighting and caterwauling that can make undesexed cats unpleasant indoor companions.

2

A girl and her cats

After beginning their married life in a cramped flat in Marrickville, Sydney, my parents bought a block of land in Turramurra in the northern suburbs. There they hoped that their three children (I was on the way at the time) would be able to grow up with fresh air and space around them. Turramurra in the 1970s was still considered 'the countryside' by many inner-city dwellers, with large blocks of land surrounded by bush and citrus fruit and pear orchards. My parents built their suburban dream home on a street that was unpaved and next door to a former farmhouse, where the Jones family lived. Mr and Mrs Jones had a number of children and, because minivans hadn't been invented yet, used to travel for holidays in a retired government bus. Mr Jones repaired lawnmowers and other machinery, and his skills must have come in handy because that old bus broke down so often that he seemed to spend a lot of his time tinkering with it to get it going again. Mr Jones also used to supplement the family income by hunting rabbits, and for this purpose he kept ferrets. The ferrets in turn attracted mice and rats so, in order to keep them under control, the Joneses acquired a ginger tomcat named Snuggy. How Snuggy got his name I have no idea, because 'snuggy' implies an adorable little animal that loves to cuddle and be cuddled. But Snuggy was not a pet. He was a 'working cat' that was expected to hunt vermin.

Snuggy, along with the unreliable bus, is one of my earliest memories. The first time I saw him I was chasing a ball that rolled down the hill of our front garden and into Mr Jones's workshop–garage. I ran to retrieve it and there I saw Snuggy, sitting on top of an old refrigerator and licking his paw. He stopped and blinked at me. I was four years old and so was he. It didn't matter to me that he was a bit rough around the

....

Still it is better, under certain circumstances, to be a cat than to be a duchess. And no duchess of the realm ever had more faithful retainers or half so abject subjects.
Helen M. Winslow (American journalist and publisher, 1851–1938)

edges, with a torn ear and scars from fights with other tomcats. It was love at first sight.

My brothers were already in school, so when my mother was busy with housework I was left to my own devices. My favourite occupation was to sit in our garden and converse with Snuggy. He must have been growing fond of me too, because he started to spend more and more time at our place. I was also the only one who could get Snuggy to come by calling his name. He soon became the subject of my crayon drawings, my first topic of conservation with strangers, and my first love.

At the time there was a little boy named Nicholas who lived in the house on the other side of us. Whenever he heard my mother backing our old Morris Minor up our steep rocky driveway (a sign that we had come home from shopping) he would climb a tree so he could wave to me over the fence. But I was not interested in Nicholas, even when he—via his mother to my mother and then to me—gave me his favourite knitted beanie. 'Wouldn't you like to go play with Nicholas?' my mother would urge. 'He likes you.' But haughty me wouldn't give Nicholas the time of day. As soon as I was out of the car, I would be running around the backyard calling out for Snuggy.

When the time came for my first day of school, I didn't cry because I missed my mother, I cried because I missed Snuggy! It took all my mother's efforts to convince me that I could not take Snuggy to school with me. So I found a temporary substitute in her wardrobe: a Russian sable fur hat that she had brought with her from China, where she had been born into the Russian community. I took the hat to school and, by placing it in the crook of my arm and making it 'breathe' with an up-and-down movement of my hand underneath, claimed to the other children—both the believing and the sceptical—that it was my cat, Snuggy. My best friend, Nicole, went along with this farce, by offering the hat her sandwich for lunch; however, one of the kindergarten teachers—I can't recall her name but let's for the sake of it call her Mrs Dragonface—put us both on detention for playing 'silly games' and deceiving the other children. Although my mother was perplexed about my obsession with Snuggy, she didn't discourage it. When we had our roast chicken on Sundays, she used to save a portion for Snuggy, which she put on his own special plate outside our back door. Snuggy, in return for this kindness, used to deposit dead rats and mice on our doormat for my mother. That didn't go down so well with her, but I think Snuggy's gratitude went most astray when he brought her a red-bellied black snake . . . still alive!

Then things took a dramatic turn. After the last of his ferrets died, Mr Jones decided to upgrade to a fox terrier named Toby. This is probably not something anyone who loves animals wants to know, least of all me, but terriers used to be employed by hunters to flush rabbits from their burrows and break their necks by shaking them. Snuggy did not like the feisty terrier and often took swipes at him, once nearly blinding the small dog. Mr Jones decided Snuggy had to go. He filled an empty petrol drum with water and took a sack from his garage, conveying to my brother that he intended to drown 'the bloody cat'. My brother told my parents and I overheard. As quickly as my legs would take me, I called Snuggy and hid with him under our house. This must have taken some courage on my part because the space under our house was my idea of 'a house of horrors'. I did not like the earthy, damp smell, the heavy gardening equipment and spare tiles my father stored in that place and I certainly did not like the idea of the deadly funnel-web spiders that my parents warned me lurked there. So there I sat in terror, cuddling Snuggy as Mr Jones looked for him, while my parents searched frantically for me.

Despite their relief at finding me, they could not coax me out of the space I had crawled into with Snuggy, no matter how hard they tried. I tearfully told them I knew of Mr Jones's dastardly plan and pleaded with them to save the cat. My mother looked at Snuggy's battle-scarred body and big tomcat head, and sighed, 'But darling, wouldn't you like a cute cuddly kitten of your own? We can get you a little kitten if you would like.'

....

It has been the providence of Nature to give
this creature nine lives instead of one.
Pilpay (Oriental fabulist, date unknown)

Dear Pebbles,

I think my new cat, Tiffany, doesn't like me. My previous cat, Jasper, used to want to be with me all the time. He used to sit on my lap, greet me when I came home, and curl up with me in bed. Tiffany, on the other hand, treats me with disdain. When I pat her she cringes; if I try to sit near her she moves away. She seems to only tolerate me when I feed her, but after that turns her nose from me and wanders off. How can I make Tiffany love me?
Rejected

Dear Rejected,

Oh dear, Rejected, I am sure Tiffany likes you far more than you realise! Your main problem is that you are comparing her to Jasper. But Tiffany is not Jasper, any more than the sky is the sea, or the moon is the sun, cats are dogs, or carob is chocolate! So to solve this problem, let Jasper rest in peace and focus on Tiffany in all her arrogant glory.

Firstly, let's rate your relationship on a scale of one to ten—from Tiffany's perspective. To do this, I want you to pick a time when she is relaxed but alert. Then slowly feign a heart attack in front of her. Give it your best now: clutch your chest, make pathetic gasping sounds and gradually collapse to the floor. Then lie as still as you can with one eye slightly open to watch what Tiffany does. If Tiffany does nothing, or simply begins to groom herself, your relationship is pretty much at the lower end of the scale, I grant you; however, if Tiffany appears at all concerned and comes and sniffs you then you are in with a fighting chance.

Women and cats are often compared to each other, and there is good reason for this. Both women and cats need to be romanced. You don't walk up to an attractive woman at a party, stick your face in hers and say, 'How about it, babe?' do you, Rejected? Do you? No, women like mystery. They like to be wooed. They do not like desperation any more than they like bad breath.

And you must never act desperate with Tiffany. This is how you win her over.

- Spritz yourself with a little eau de catnip. Catnip contains nepetalactone, which can create a sense of euphoria and overwhelming happiness in many cats. If catnip is not Tiffany's thing, try a synthetic cat pheromone product. Go easy with it, though; just as with aftershave, sometimes less is more.
- Be mysterious. Play a little hard to get. Don't be all over Tiffany like a rash. Sit in her presence and simply read a book. After a while she will wonder why you are paying more attention to the book than to her.
- Get down on the floor. This is quite irresistible to a cat. Read on the floor. Lie on a yoga mat and stare at the ceiling.

This will give you that *je ne sais quoi* that might just turn the corner for you and Tiffany.

- ♥ Don't stare at her, no matter how beautiful she is. In the cat world this is as off-putting as a human man ogling a woman's bosom. Instead, when you look at her, slowly blink. It's flirtatious and alluring.
- ♥ Don't grope her; rather, beckon her with an open hand. Allow her to sniff your fingers before you even think of touching her.
- ♥ Share a romantic dinner. You eat yours while she eats hers next to you.
- ♥ Give her little surprises, such as a cat treat, for no reason other than that you love her. Give her these gifts unexpectedly and no more than two or three times a week. You'll increase her sense of anticipation when she sees you.
- ♥ Play with her. Discover what games she likes—perhaps a tickle with a feather, perhaps a little sparkly thing on the end of a pole, perhaps a cute toy mouse that she can rip to shreds.
- ♥ Does Tiffany like to be brushed? If she does, brush her often and get to know her special spots.

If you take time to woo Tiffany you might just find that she has fallen in love with you and, before long, she will sit in your lap voluntarily, welcome you home and snuggle with you on the sofa.

Pebbles

I firmly shook my head and my parents went away to discuss the matter, returning with some biscuits. Even the warm sugary smell of them could not coax me out. Seeing they were defeated, my mother told me, 'All right, I'll get your father to speak to Mr Jones.' I strained my ears to listen to the conversation my father had with Mr Jones in his front yard, knowing that the fate of Snuggy hung in the balance. Mr Jones's anger at Snuggy seemed to have calmed somewhat and, while I didn't catch every word of the conversation, I did hear his surprised grunt when my father offered him money for us to take Snuggy off his hands. Mr Jones agreed and when my mother told me the news my heart burst with joy: Snuggy was now officially mine!

Life for the tomcat was about to change in ways he probably could never have imagined. My mother bought Snuggy some matching purple dishes with fish painted on them and my father built him a cat bed. He got his own brush set and was introduced to the joys of flea powder and worming paste. And that wasn't all that was going to change. To stop him spraying and to curb his aggressive habit of scratching everyone but me, he was going to have to be desexed. At that time, it was quite unusual for people to take their cats to veterinarians and there certainly weren't any fancy cat carriers as there are today, in every style and colour imaginable. If you did take your cat to the vet, it was usually in a cardboard box with airholes punched in it. We tried that with Snuggy but within two minutes he had torn the box to shreds and all that was left was our cat

Cat wisdom

Sylvester

*'Let me tell you a secret: curiosity did not kill the cat;
boredom did. Do you know what I'm saying?'*

✳ ✳ ✳

sitting triumphantly on a cardboard platform. Then my father,
a mechanical engineer, had the idea of placing one washing
basket on top of another and tying the two together. We all
marvelled at his ingenuity, especially as Snuggy would 'be able
to see out', not quite realising then that Snuggy being able to
see out was perhaps not such a good idea.

The only veterinary surgery near us was on top of a bicycle
shop in the refined part of Turramurra where people lived in
Federation mansions with tennis courts and heated swimming
pools. The practice had recently been established by a dashing
young veterinarian with the unfortunate surname of Meany.
We bustled into the waiting room with Snuggy growling in

the washing basket, to find ourselves faced with the horrified looks of the Upper North Shore matrons sitting there with their well-behaved Persians.

Doctor Meany himself was alarmed and thought that we had brought him a feral cat to euthanise. When my parents set him straight on that matter, he took them aside and asked, 'Wouldn't your little girl prefer a kitten from a prestige breeder?' My parents had to go through the same explanation they had given equally perturbed friends: 'No, our daughter wants this cat.'

Once Snuggy was 'done', he quickly settled into the life of an adored companion. (Oddly enough, the fortunes of his nemesis, Toby the terrier, changed at the same time. Mr Jones sadly died in his sleep one night and the fox terrier was retired from rabbit hunting and elevated to kindly Mrs Jones's highly indulged lapdog. His rabbit-hunting days were over for good).

Now I was old enough to write, I filled exercise books and notepads with stories, poems and songs about Snuggy. He was my muse and my inspiration. He didn't protest about my flair for the theatrical either, and sat patiently as I dressed him in various costumes—a Hawaiian hula girl being a favourite—and then pushed him around in a pram. Then one day when I was six, I put a bow tie around Snuggy's neck, placed my mother's wedding veil on my head and solemnly 'married' him. Life as newlyweds was blissful for Snuggy and me for the next few years, with the occasional hiccup; such as when my mother caught me and my friend Margaret eating Snuggy's dried biscuits during a highly elaborate garden tea party we had set up with my cat as the guest of honour.

When I was eight years old my parents thought I might be spending too much time inside and decided to get me a bicycle so I could join in with the neighbourhood children, riding around the hilly streets of Turramurra. I was taken to the bicycle shop under Dr Meany's Veterinary Surgery to choose a model. Two weeks later the shop called to say that my bicycle had arrived and we could come and pick it up. As any new acquisition was a family affair, my brothers planned to come too. My parents, my brother, Paul, and I got into our new bright orange Leyland Marina and waited for my brother, Chris, to join us. He appeared from around the corner of the house frowning. He asked my mother to wind down her window and he whispered something to her. My mother got out and after a few minutes returned with a box, which she put on her lap. 'Snuggy isn't well,' she said, calmly. 'Your brothers and I will take him to the vet while you get your bicycle with your father.' I wanted to look at Snuggy to see what was the matter with him but she told me he was sleeping and not to disturb him. She assured me Snuggy would be fine and just needed Dr Meany to look at him 'because he has a cold'. I had come to think of my cat as invincible so I didn't even suspect there was anything seriously wrong.

Apart from a bout of pneumonia that had put me in hospital for six weeks, nothing had ever gone badly wrong in my short

innocent life. My father and I arrived at the bicycle shop and there was my sparkly pink Malvern Star with a petal-patterned seat waiting for me. The shop manager adjusted the seat for me and I gave it a test ride in the parking lot at the back of the shop. While my father was paying for the bicycle, I rushed out of the shop before he could stop me and ran up the stairs to Dr Meany's surgery, keen to tell Snuggy all about the new bicycle. I had a fantasy about riding around with him in the front basket. But before I reached the second floor my mother came out of the veterinary surgery. She didn't have Snuggy in his box in her hands. She was crying.

A strange sensation crept over my skin, but I couldn't make any sense of it. 'Snuggy?'

My mother tried to say something, but she couldn't. She shook her head. My brothers came out of the surgery and looked at each other when they saw me, standing frozen on the landing.

Chris stepped towards me. 'Snuggy was very sick. He had a tumour. The vet said he was suffering, so he put him to sleep.'

I shook my head, not comprehending. If he was asleep, then he would wake up, wouldn't he? When the truth dawned, a wave of excruciating pain washed over me. I was breathless with it. I hadn't known anyone who had died, apart from Mr Jones. Snuggy was my first crushing loss. I didn't want anything to do with my new bicycle, associating its arrival with Snuggy's sudden departure. For the next few weeks, each afternoon when

I came home from school I would stand at the bottom of the driveway and squint at the front garden, as if by the strength of my will I could make Snuggy appear again. He would rub against my legs and follow me into the house as he had done for the past few years. But he didn't reappear, and I refused to go to Sunday School, fiercely angry at God. How could he have taken from me the thing I loved most? Even the promise of a young kitten couldn't bring me solace.

It would be years later, when I suffered a sudden tragic loss, that I would recall the intense grief I had felt over Snuggy. I didn't go through the denial or bargaining stage that second time; I accepted the event immediately. Snuggy's death had shown me that no matter how much you love someone, how deeply you wish to hold on, when someone dies, they are gone. They don't come back. You have to let them go.

But Snuggy taught me something else: that the love always remains. Even as I think of my first cat now, all these years later, a warm glow fills my heart. The love is still there and always will be. A bond like that lasts forever; even death cannot break it.

Florence Nightingale

ENGLISH HUMANITARIAN AND FOUNDER
OF MODERN NURSING (1820–1910)

Florence Nightingale derived comfort from the companionship of her feline friends when she returned from the Crimean War with her health in ruins. Indefatigable despite her chronic ailments, Nightingale authored books on nursing and lobbied for better hospital planning. Owning more than sixty cats over her lifetime, she wrote with her numerous feline companions wandering around her writing desk, knocking over inkpots and leaving footprints on hospital reports and letters. Despite all her efforts for humanity and having numerous honours bestowed on her by royalty, Nightingale spent the last years of her life alone, never leaving her bedroom, which overlooked the Dorchester flower garden. Her cats were her greatest consolation, more faithful to her than humans. In honour of their loyalty, she made provision for their continued care and upkeep in her will.

Cat love

After Snuggy passed away and my parents saw that I had no interest in my new bicycle, they took me to the RSPCA and told me to select a kitten. I peered into a wire cage to see a litter of black-and-grey-striped kittens clambering over one another and mock-fighting with their minuscule paws. In the corner, as regal as Cleopatra, sat one tiny kitten. Her front paws, chest and a third of her face were the purest white, while the tortoiseshell colouring on the crown of her head and down her back were a combination of crème caramel and silver grey. She was gorgeous! I pointed to her and one of the volunteers lifted her tail—rather unceremoniously for such an elegant cat—to check her sex and announced that she was a girl, as most cats with tortoiseshell colouring are. She was placed into my arms and I pressed my cheek to her velvety head.

'What are you going to call her?' my mother asked. 'She's beautiful!'

'Stunning!' my father agreed.

Indeed she absolutely was. Her golden eyes were rimmed with a thick line of kohl-like markings that extended from the outer lids to her ears. She could have been an Egyptian cat goddess worthy of a name like Bastet or Isis.

I named her . . . Fluffy! (It was the title of a favourite book.)

So this beautiful cat, who could have descended from the heavens, came to be the centre of my quirky, middle-class family. I was thrilled when my parents told me that she could sleep in my bed with me when she was a little bit bigger, a pleasure they had drawn the line at with Snuggy. I was in love with her. Never having had a sister and always having wanted one, I adopted her into that role. I read to her, told stories to her and played dress-ups with her. My childhood friend Nicole (the same one who fed her sandwich to my mother's hat) tells me that every birthday and Christmas card I ever sent to her was always signed, 'Belinda and Fluffy XX'. Although she was essentially my cat, she was adored by everyone, especially my mother. Premium pet foods were not available then so my mother used to make Fluffy her own combinations of human-grade mince meat with an egg yolk mixed in as well as some wheatgerm, brewer's yeast and cat vitamins to make sure she

---

Refined and delicate natures understand the cat.
Women, poets, and artists hold it in great esteem ...
only coarse natures fail to discern the natural
distinction of the animal.
Champfleury (French art critic and novelist, 1821–1889)

got enough taurine, which cats' bodies don't manufacture on their own. (This was fed to her alongside a commercial cat food. Purely homemade diets are fraught with the risk of vitamin deficiencies.) Once a week she was given a small amount of raw liver or tuna. I think my homemaker mum was glad for the company while we were all at work or school.

My father, too, doted on her. Having witnessed a pet kitten killed by a dog when he was a small boy, he'd never been able to risk opening his heart again to an animal until Fluffy came along. Now he was constantly carting her around to show her various aspects of the garden and forever designing more elaborate cat beds and 'lookouts' for her. And my brothers never shirked their share of her care. My eldest brother combed her to make sure she didn't collect fleas, while my other brother made sure that she was always inside by her sundown curfew.

Cats bring love into a home. They do indeed become members of our families. According to biologist Bruce H. Lipton, love is the most powerful energy we can have flowing through our bodies. It is our life force, our *chi*. While anger, fear and worry lower our immune systems, opening us up to disease, love heals us: mind, body and spirit. It doesn't matter whether that energy is shared with another human being or an animal. It is especially important that we give healthy doses of it to ourselves. It is all love.

One of the biggest changes in my home town of Sydney in recent years has been the 'Manhattanisation' of the city. More and more people are choosing to live in apartments rather than the traditional Australian freestanding house with a garden. Families are shrinking to two parents and a child, or a single parent and one or two children.

'Children are becoming disconnected from nature and more attached to technology,' Halina Thompson, president of the World League for Protection of Animals (WLPA), says. 'I always tell parents to encourage their child to read to their cat and to tell them all their secrets. Getting their child to share in simple caring tasks—making sure that the water in their cat's drinking bowl is refreshed every day, or brushing their cat to prevent furballs—is a way of getting them to break out of their own little worlds and to think about the needs of others.'

Fluffy was certainly a very special childhood friend to me. She would walk to the end of the driveway with me when I set off for school and would be waiting there when I came home. I could tell her things I couldn't bring myself to tell my mother, such as about bullying and hurtful name-calling at school. She would always be a gentle listener with those watchful golden eyes. She was also my consolation when I got older and teenage angst was the order of the day. She was with me as I grew from a girl to a young woman who was about to go to university in California. I watched Fluffy change too, from a playful kitten to a matronly queen, to a frail old lady. Knowing that Fluffy didn't have much time left, I wanted to delay my trip to California. She was loyal to me and I was loyal to her. In the end she passed away two months before I had to leave, when her kidney disease progressed to the point that her quality of life was diminishing. The night after she was put to sleep, I felt her jump onto the bed and curl up to me. Many cat lovers talk about similar experiences with their deceased feline companions. People have all sorts of explanations for this; I suggest you go with your own.

Often as 'cat women' we are made to feel embarrassed about loving our cats. Love is love. Just because we love our cats doesn't mean we don't love our spouses, children or parents, or that we don't care for other human beings, or want to make the world a better place. But interspecies love is a very special, sacred thing. Every woman who has loved a cat knows that.

Guardian angels

In medieval times cats were called the 'familiars' of witches. A familiar is an animal with which you have a deep spiritual connection; one who can act as your link between the physical and spiritual realms. If we take the view that all

life is intertwined, and that we are all souls having a physical experience, then it makes sense that the animal companions we have at certain periods of our lives are there for a purpose. They have been sent to teach us, guide us, comfort us, or help us to grow and develop in some way. That perfectly describes my relationship with my beautiful cream Burmese cats, Gardenia and Lilac.

They came into my life at a time when I had returned to Australia after working in New York. Since my childhood companion cat, Fluffy, had passed away nine years earlier I had led a nomadic existence: living and working in different cities and having a philosophy of not owning more than I could fit into two suitcases. I wanted to be mobile; I wanted to travel light. All that changed for me in 2001. While in New York I had written my first novel, *White Gardenia*. Although I felt called to be a writer, everything I had submitted for the past ten years had been rejected: short stories, articles, a novel and a nonfiction book. I don't think I even got a 'letter to the editor' published, but I kept going.

I missed Fluffy's company at those times when after work, or in the early hours of the morning, I opened my laptop, lit a lavender-scented candle and sipped a cup of steaming green tea before commencing work on my impossible dream. I did have the company of my flatmate's cat, the whisper-light black Sabine who used to sit so quietly on my lap that I barely noticed she was there. I loved New York and the vibrant people I met there, but the personality I missed most on returning to Sydney was Sabine. I'll never forget her little face, pressed against the front window of the apartment, as I got into the taxi for the run to JFK Airport on the day that I was leaving. My heart ached and if she hadn't had such a doting cat-mother in my flatmate, I would have taken her with me!

I'd had an inkling that there was something special about *White Gardenia*, but I did not expect it to become the runaway success that it did. It was sold in a competitive auction deal,

which resulted in a two-book contract, and suddenly—presto!—
I was a full-time writer. My priorities changed overnight: I
wanted somewhere permanent to write. I longed for a garden to
tend and a social circle that wasn't full of exotic internationals
on temporary working visas. But most of all I wanted a cat
of my own, or two in this case. Perhaps two cats to keep me
settled would be the replacement for the two suitcases that
had kept me on the move.

It was before my animal activist days, something Gardenia
and Lilac were to influence. I wasn't aware of the sheer number
of cats in shelters and pounds that face grim futures if they
aren't adopted. I understood the most responsible thing to do
was to obtain my cats from a reputable breeder rather than
a pet shop, so I set about researching different cat breeds.
I settled on Burmese because they were renowned for their
bright personalities and playfulness. My initial plan was to
acquire a boy and a girl cat but all that changed on the day
that I met Lilac.

I found a breeder, Robin, in Ourimbah on the New South
Wales Central Coast. She had a litter of three cream Burmese
female kittens and selected one of them for me to come and see.
Entering her home, I immediately became aware that the cats
she bred were brought up in an environment of privilege. It was
winter and the heating was set to a toasty 30 degrees Celsius,
Bach was softly playing in the background and a DVD of
swimming goldfish flickered from the television in the corner.

Cat wisdom

Farrah

'Do you think a cat ever worries if she is beautiful? Does she ever stop to wonder if she is good enough? Thin enough? Nice enough? No, because we love ourselves just as we are—fluffy or short-haired; fat or slim; white or black. No matter what our size, breed or temperament, we think we are the cat's whiskers. You are beautiful and perfect as you are too: celebrate your uniqueness!'

✳ ✳ ✳

As well as Burmese, Robin raised Russian blues. Her own grand female Russian blue eyed me with all the haughtiness of a tsarina as I passed by her. The kittens were kept in netted tents in the living room so that they wouldn't accidentally get underfoot or become trapped behind furniture. 'They are handled several times a day by all the family members,' Robin explained. 'That way they get used to people of all ages and grow up into friendly cats.' Before she would show me the kitten she was considering for me, she sat me down for what was essentially an interview.

I sat on the edge of my chair, like an eager adoptive parent, answering questions about my ability to provide the kind of life for which Robin's kittens had clearly been bred. After I had assured her I had the funds for my kitten's veterinary care, that she would be kept indoors full time (except for a saunter around the garden on a walking lead), that I would have her desexed and vaccinated, and that I would feed her only the strict diet Robin prescribed for her, I was handed the kitten's pedigree papers to examine her lineage and purebred status. It was so far removed from the way I had acquired Snuggy and Fluffy that I felt like I was marrying into the British royal family.

After viewing the kitten's parents, a regal pair, I was informed that I would only be able to take my kitten home after she reached six months of age. According to Robin, that's how long it would take for her personality to 'stabilise' and for her 'schooling' by her natural mother and the other adult female cats in the household to be completed. Then I finally got to meet my kitten. Going by her show name of 'La Crème', she was lounging in a sheepskin cat bed with her sister. She was every bit as gorgeous as you would expect her to be, given the surroundings. Robin picked her up and placed her in my arms. I was immediately taken by her muscular compact body, her silky caramel and cream fur, and her beautiful round face with its petal pink nose and golden eyes. That she had 'personality', I had no doubt. If a cat could smile, La Crème was certainly smiling in a way that suggested she might be thinking, 'Hello! Yes, I am rather beautiful, don't you think?' Robin explained that La Crème's sister had already been spoken for by a couple in Rose Bay who had obviously met the 'cat-parenting' requirements.

Something nudged my ankle and I looked down to see another Burmese kitten looking up at me. It was the third sister. She was more oriental in her physique than her siblings with a sleeker body and a chiselled, slightly wedge-shaped head. Her fur was fawn coloured, but blended through it around her mask, tail and ears was a pretty shade of shimmery lilac. The thing that struck me most was her eyes: they sparkled with ethereal beauty.

'Oh, that's "Royal Storm", my naughty tortie,' explained Robin, scooping her up and holding her up to her face. 'Her colour is perfection. She's my husband's favourite. I'm going to keep her for breeding.' But whichever way Robin turned, the little kitten did not take her eyes from me. Robin put her back in the tent and gave her a gentle shove.

We sat down together to do La Crème's change of ownership paperwork, when I felt another nudge at my ankle. I looked down and there was the lilac kitten again.

Robin glanced over the top of her glasses. 'Goodness me, look at that. Royal Storm is completely taken with you. She normally doesn't show such an interest in people.'

I looked at Royal Storm and she peered back at me. Something stirred in my heart: this kitten and I were meant to meet. I had been planning to search for a chocolate Burmese boy cat from another breeder, but all thoughts of that slipped out of my head. 'Do you think I could take her too?' I asked.

Robin hesitated, and then nodded. 'Sometimes it just happens like that. A cat chooses a person.'

So I left Ourimbah that day with a skip in my step. I would have to wait two more months before the two cats I had decided to call Gardenia (because she was so glorious and creamy) and Lilac (because with the shimmer of pink-grey through her fur there seemed no other choice) could come and live with me. I stuck their pictures on my refrigerator and glanced at them every morning with all the surprise, joy and excitement of someone falling in love. I must have sensed that a great and wonderful journey was about to unfold.

....

[A] kitten is in the animal world what the rosebud is in the garden.
Robert Southey (English poet laureate, 1774–1843)

Dear Pebbles,

I am at my wit's end with my cat, Twinkles. She is a hardcore shredder. She has torn my drapes, turned my Louis XV rococo sofa into a piece of postmodernist art, and now she is scratching my bedposts. A friend of mine suggested that I squirt her with a water pistol when I catch her scratching anything. Now Twinkles runs away from me whenever I come home, or she hides under the bed. It hasn't stopped her scratching though. Yesterday I discovered she had started scratching the legs of my Italian baroque dining table. I love Twinkles and wonder if I should just give in and live in an apartment that looks like Jackson Pollock decorated it?
Frustrated

Dear Frustrated,

Oh no! I do not think you should give up on having your apartment as you like it or see any reason why you and Twinkles can't live together as harmoniously as Joséphine Bonaparte and her orangutan at the Château de Malmaison. You are experiencing a classic communication clash between the human and feline species. What you describe as 'naughty' behaviour is as vital to Twinkles' wellbeing as home ownership, a lock on the door, and dinner-party planning is to you.

Let me explain: territory is of utmost importance to we cats. One of the ways we mark ours is to leave scratches and the pheromones from our paws on objects we wish to stake as our territory; in the wild, usually on trees. These scratches and scents are the equivalent of signs that proclaim 'Private Property of Twinkles. Keep Out!' We also scratch to release an inner build-up of emotion in the same way you might sing, dance or play the ukulele. Have you noticed that Twinkles often scratches right after you come home? She's not scratching your sofa to annoy you. She is telling you, 'I'm so excited to see you! I anticipate that something wonderful is going to happen!' And then what do you do? You squirt her with a shot of water! Can you see how this is playing with her mind? No wonder she is confused and hiding from you.

I might add that Twinkles is not marking territory against you. She includes you in her territory which is why she marks you by rubbing herself against your legs. Your sofa is soaked with the scent of the naps you have taken together on it and the nights you have binge-watched Netflix with Twinkles asleep on your lap. It is a place of great sentimental value to Twinkles. That's why she has included it in her special territory.

So now that you understand why Twinkles scratches things, here's what you can do. Firstly, do not get angry at her. She does not associate your negative behaviour with anything she has done; rather, she thinks you have lost your marbles. Cats are like sensitive children: we respond better to positive redirection than punishment. Twinkles needs a cat scratcher, but not just any cat scratcher.

Firstly is she mainly a horizontal scratcher or a vertical scratcher? In your case it sounds like she is a vertical scratcher. Horizontal scratchers are felines that use the carpet or rugs to mark their territory. So get Twinkles a post. Most cats like sisal the best. Make sure it is tall enough for Twinkles to fully stretch herself out on and sturdy at the base. She will not use a scratcher if it wobbles. You could get her a horizontal scratcher as well, as she might appreciate the variety.

'But I got her a scratcher!' I hear you protest. 'It's a lovely one in the Louis XV style, but she doesn't use it!'

Well, firstly, Frustrated, where did you put it? If you put it in the spare room that's next to useless. You must put the scratcher where you and Twinkles spend most of your time together; for instance, next to your sofa. The next thing, please do not tell me that when you installed it that you grabbed Twinkles' paws and rubbed them up and down on it to show her what you wanted her to do? No! No! No! When you give your mother-in-law a Christmas present do you watch her unwrap it then grab both her hands and place them on the gift and say, 'There, Betty, this is your new Mixmaster!' Do you pull her fingers and direct them to use the controls? Your mother-in-law would think you were insane, and Twinkles does too when you engage in that sort of demeaning behaviour. Twinkles is not a dog!

The best way to get Twinkles interested in her new scratcher is to scratch it yourself. The sound of nails running down a sisal post is as irresistible to a feline as the sound of someone crunching potato chips (or, to the more discerning among us, the sound of the caramelised top of a crème brûlèe being cracked). She will be intrigued. Also, if you rub your socks over it along with a clean sock that you have rubbed against her cheeks to collect her pheromones, it will carry the scent of all those happy times you have spent together on your sofa. A spritz of catnip mist and a cat treat perched at the top of the post will entice her to explore. As a final touch, place her favourite toys around the base of it. And, most importantly, when she does scratch the post instead of your sofa, praise her!

Pebbles

P.S. And use that water pistol on your friend instead!

As kittens, Gardenia and Lilac were active as monkeys, more mischievous together than perhaps they would have been on their own. They'd bolt around the house, chasing each other, sliding across the floor and even clambering up walls. Until they were two years old I don't think there was a painting in my house that ever hung straight. They were like a pair of mountain lions in their insatiable thirst for heights. When I couldn't find them, I didn't look under chairs or under the bed but up on top of cupboards or even precariously balanced on top of doors. I trained them to walk on leads, as Robin had instructed, but on our first venture outdoors, rather than the orderly stroll I expected, I ended up with two kittens scrambling up to the top of a four-metre tree, their walking leads trailing behind them. I thought I was going to have to call the fire brigade until they managed to climb down nimbly by themselves.

Robin said that their personalities would 'stabilise' by six months of age and while the two sisters did everything from sitting on windowsills to walking upstairs as a perfectly synchronised pair, they couldn't have been more different.

Lilac, despite having the show name 'Royal Storm', was lady-like. She had a dainty walk and a prance-like run. Slim, graceful and full of poise and elegant charm, she was a feline version of Audrey Hepburn. Gardenia was Mae West. Supremely confident, bold and flirtatious, she always assumed that anyone who came to visit the house had come to see her. If a courier arrived at the door, Gardenia would rush over, rubbing at the courier's legs and blinking her come-hither eyes. Journalists, plumbers, painters, computer technicians and piano tuners were all treated to her bewitchery. She was pure Hollywood diva.

One evening I invited some friends back for a cup of tea after the theatre. As soon as Gardenia heard their voices when we came into the house, she was at the top of the stairs. My guests disappeared into the living room but I lingered in the hall to witness Gardenia's entry firsthand. First she perked up with a look in her eye that said, 'All right, Mr DeMille, I am ready for my close-up.' She sauntered down the stairs, but she didn't enter the living room right away. She sat in the doorway a moment until one of the female guests noticed her and said, 'Oh, what a beautiful cat.' The room went silent and everyone turned to look at Gardenia, and only then did she slink into the room and greet each guest individually. If she had turned into a human at that moment she would have been a buxom blonde in a sequined dress with a tiara in her hair and a cigarette in a holder. 'Fabulous party, darling, isn't it?' would have purred from her lips. She was magnetism on four paws. I was in awe of her.

Gardenia and Lilac slept together on a pillow on my desk while I wrote, sometimes purring, sometimes snoring, sometimes dreaming with little twitches and chirrups as they chased imaginary birds. Their presence is woven into many of my stories. It's there in the friendships between characters, the quiet moments and in the sad partings. Gardenia influenced Natalya Azarova's bold personality in *Sapphire Skies*, while Lilac was the inspiration for Kira, Simone de Fleurier's good-luck mascot in *Wild Lavender*. Kira was a Russian blue in the story but every inch of her personality was Lilac's, especially her love of anything sparkly, sequined or made of satin. Not one of my ballroom gowns, dance shoes or evening dresses was safe around her.

Kira jumped from my stomach and tugged one of my ballet slippers along the carpet by its ribbons. She wasn't a destructive cat, but silky or shiny things were her weakness. If I didn't put them away, my underwear and earrings were always going missing, only to be found later in Kira's food dish.

I loved my personality-plus cats, but our bond—the deep connection we were to share—happened one freezing July night, when my mother died unexpectedly. My father had undergone major heart surgery the month before: he was the one we were all worrying about. I had not expected to lose my mother, especially without any warning. She had been the most important influence in my life, the person closest to me, and my greatest supporter. Then suddenly she was gone. I returned from the emergency room at the hospital, where I'd kissed her goodbye and told her I loved her, and sat alone at home shivering. It was two o'clock in the morning, too early to call anyone, and I couldn't get warm. I turned the heating on, tugged on two jumpers and covered myself in a winter-weight quilt, but my teeth wouldn't stop chattering. I was in shock. Gardenia and Lilac, sensing the gravity of the situation, came and sat on top of me, watching me with their concerned eyes. In the following days and weeks, as the funeral was organised and my grieving began in earnest, they curbed their rascally behaviour. Wherever I was in the house, they would come and sit with me, quietly and calmly. They made no demands for food or to play. Overnight they changed from hyperactive cats to watchful guardian angels.

Healing energy

Love is the most expansive energy any of us can experience. There is some research into how love—especially healthy self-love—might be able to help heal the human body. Love is not a finite thing. Loving a person—or an animal—opens your heart to loving other people and animals. The very nature of love means that it is constantly expanding, constantly opening us up to more love. In loving Gardenia and Lilac, my heart began to open to the plight of other animals. I lived in a bushland area and on my way to and from an evening dance class I travelled on a road that went through a national park. --→

It would break my heart to see the roadkill of native animals on my way back home, their lifeless bodies scattered over the verge and tarmac as if they were nothing more than rubbish. If Lilac and Gardenia were precious with their own unique personalities, then these animals were precious too, and should be treated as such. That heartbreak led me to becoming involved in the local wildlife group, rescuing and rehabilitating injured wildlife.

I met amazing people through that organisation. I also began to think more deeply about the treatment of farm animals and decided to become a vegetarian and be more conscious in my choice of clothing and cosmetics. Sometimes we are afraid to change something in our lifestyle that would benefit another, wondering where our altruism might take us. But conscious living—while having its challenges—always opens us up more to life and takes us beyond ourselves. A lot of the time we worry that we can't be perfect in our lifestyle choices: we say, 'I'm conscious about ethically made clothing, but I have to drive to work' and so on. My mantra on this is to start somewhere, even if it is something as simple as using a drink bottle instead of buying water in plastic containers. Small differences start to add up.

When Gardenia and Lilac were four years old, Lilac began having severe bouts of vomiting and diarrhoea. I had just moved to a new part of Sydney and at first the veterinarian thought it might have been the change of address that had caused it: 'It doesn't take much to upset a cat's apple cart,' he said. When she didn't improve, I sought a second opinion.

The new veterinarian, Marilyn, was careful in her examination and ordered an ultrasound. 'She has a mass in her intestine,' she informed me. 'We have to get it out. It's right where her large and small intestines meet.'

A mass on an ultrasound is not something anybody wants to hear about. On the day I took Lilac for her surgery, I placed a rose quartz bracelet my mother had given me in her cat carrier. The nurse assured me she would be well taken care of, but my heart broke just the same when I went home to await the news. The veterinarian who operated called later to say that the mass had been successfully removed and the pathology showed that it wasn't cancer. I breathed a sigh of relief when he told me that I would be able to pick her up the following day. But when Lilac didn't recover sufficiently to be taken home, Marilyn was concerned. 'She should be feeling better by now and I'm worried that she isn't.' She performed a needle biopsy and called me to say that Lilac needed emergency surgery. 'Her gut isn't holding,' she told me, 'and she is in danger of septicaemia.'

I hadn't moved from the telephone when Marilyn called again half an hour later. 'Her intestine doesn't look like it's going to hold. It's coming apart and we can't find any healthy tissue. We will try to save her, but prepare for the worst.'

I put down the receiver in a state of shock. How could this have happened to dainty Lilac? I couldn't lose her so young! I put my head in my hands, understanding everything was out of my control. What became clear at that moment was that I had no spiritual source to call on.

I had been brought up with a Christian education but, while I have the deepest respect for people whose religious faith inspires them to works of compassion, I had found Christianity to be oppressively patriarchal. It had been very damaging to my young woman's psyche to be told that I was to be submissive to men and that, through Eve, women were responsible for all that was evil in the world. I also couldn't believe that good people would be condemned to burn in hell, simply because they didn't hold a certain set of beliefs. So I had drifted away.

Now it seemed that as my darling cat lay on the operating table, and my own emotional and mental resources were drained, I had nothing higher to call on. Desperate for something, I dialled the only spiritual person I knew then, a wonderful woman I used to work with, a spiritual healer named Maggie. I telephoned her and sobbed into the receiver.

'Who is this?' she asked.

Cat wisdom

Milo

'Black cats are constantly told we are "unlucky". But the genes that give us our colour also give us superstar immune systems and increase our longevity! We also look slim even when we are fat. I'd call that pretty lucky! Your "faults" are often your greatest strengths.'

✳ ✳ ✳

When I explained that my cat was dying and asked her to pray for us, she told me very gently, 'Belinda, you can't hold on to her. If it's her time to go, even if she is young, you have to let her go.'

So I did. I closed my eyes and imagined Lilac. I told her that if it was her time to go I would let her go. I loved her and always would.

The telephone rang a few minutes later. It was Marilyn. 'The most amazing thing happened!' she said, her voice filled with relief. 'Lilac's tissue seemed to come to life before our eyes. We've managed to close the wound.'

Lilac took a long time to recover. She was in hospital for three weeks. I visited her every day, comforting her and stroking her. She returned my affection, but she wasn't eating on her own and that was a problem. I dreaded waking up every morning to make my call to the veterinary surgery, terrified I would be informed that she had passed away overnight. Then one morning, my eyes fluttered open to see my mother standing next to the bed. 'Belinda,' she said, 'Don't worry, everything is going to be all right.' A sense of peace washed over me; I fell back asleep and dreamed I was walking down a dark corridor. At the end of it was a door with a sliver of light shining out from the bottom of it. I reached the door and pushed it slowly open. I was almost blinded by the flash of white light that emanated from the room. An angel stood there cradling Lilac in his arms. I woke up to find the sun was shining into my bedroom. I had slept past my usual waking time. I called the veterinary surgery and the nurse there told me excitedly that Lilac had started eating on her own and if she continued she wouldn't have to be fed through the tube.

After that, I referred to Lilac as my 'little miracle cat'. The incident with Lilac's operation taught me that begging the Divine for what we want doesn't invite miracles; trust and surrender do. I believe that every person or animal appears in our life for a reason. It was due to Lilac's near death that I began to explore spiritualism that wasn't tied to any religion, and that faith has served me well. It has brought me comfort in many difficult circumstances since and has also allowed me to experience the magic in the subtleties of life.

Gardenia and Lilac were to be my writing companions for nearly sixteen years, through six sprawling historical novels— *Wild Lavender, Silver Wattle, Tuscan Rose, Golden Earrings, Sapphire Skies* and *Southern Ruby*. It was while I was working on *Southern Ruby* that I learned that my now elderly Lilac's kidneys were starting to deteriorate. Since her operation she had been diagnosed with a severe form of inflammatory bowel disease. This meant that she had a special diet along with daily medication and regular visits to the Sydney University Vet and Emergency Clinic, where she was looked after by renowned feline specialist Professor Vanessa Barrs and her team of specialist vets. Lilac had done well for so many years and now it seemed her life was coming to a close. My sorrow is there in the character of Ruby in *Southern Ruby*, who so desperately doesn't want to lose her ailing mother.

I'm often asked by readers if I ever revisit my books, but I rarely do, because in between the lines of the story I remember what was happening at that time in my life. *Wild Lavender* mourns the loss of my mother, and *Southern Ruby* reminds me of a long, hard goodbye: two in fact. I was only just coming to terms with Lilac's failing health, when I received more terrible news. One weekend, Gardenia, who had always been robustly healthy, started to have trouble breathing. She'd just had a 'senior's check' a few weeks before and her blood-test results had all been normal so I thought that she might have gotten pneumonia. But an X-ray revealed fluid in her lungs and a follow-up ultrasound revealed lymphoma. As the veterinarian read out to me each of the places they had found tumours in her digestive system, it was like having a new bullet shot into me. How could Gardenia, always so energetic and youthful in appearance, be so dreadfully sick? I was told that the fluid in her lungs could build up again at any time and I'd have to have her put to sleep in the next couple of days. Back at home, I lay on my bed with Gardenia and Lilac asleep under my arms and watched the sunset. How could this be? How could I be losing these two dear friends at the same time?

I emailed Professor Barrs to tell her the news and she wrote straight back to me. 'Bring her in tomorrow. Lymphoma of the digestive tract can often be sent into remission with mild chemotherapy. Gastric lymphoma is the better of the lymphomas to have.'

When I arrived at the university the following day, the cancer specialist explained to me that the chemotherapy used on cats is milder than the dose given to humans and Gardenia wouldn't get sick or suffer drastic side effects. They would not be able to cure the disease, but they might be able to send it into remission for another six months, perhaps even a year if we were extra lucky. Six months was all that Lilac had been given. I wanted the two sisters to remain together for as long as possible.

So after that, it was weekly visits for both Gardenia and Lilac to the university vet hospital. They had done everything together since they were kittens and it seemed they were going to make this last journey together too. Both responded extremely well to the care they received. While Lilac did start to lose weight and look frail, Gardenia never changed. In fact, she seemed to look forward to the hospital visits because of all the attention she received!

Each afternoon I would set Gardenia and Lilac up in the sunniest part of the house. There we would all nap together or I would write while they slept peacefully. Every moment of those last months together was precious and sacred. We were all moving through a transition. As it turned out, Lilac did well for another year until she developed diabetes from her medication and started to lose too much weight to sustain herself. On the morning before the veterinarian was due to come to put her to sleep at home, Gardenia and Lilac ate a meal together then happily snuggled up on the bed side by side. I watched them with a heart that was breaking, but that was so full of love. Gardenia's remission lasted much longer than six months. To everyone's surprise she remained as robust and as cheeky as ever for another year and a half. Although the loss of Lilac had left a gaping hole in my heart, Gardenia was an enormous comfort to me. She was still running up and down stairs and leaping from windowsills and keeping my rescue cat, Gucci, in his place until her last day—my birthday—when she suddenly collapsed. A small tumour had returned and burst. She had to be put to sleep the next morning. I kissed her soft honey-smelling forehead and thanked her for all the times we had shared together and told her how much she had enriched my life, and then she was gone too.

The grief I felt at the loss of Gardenia and Lilac was deep and painful. I had devoted myself to their care for so long, it was as though a part of me had gone too. I was fortunate to have beautiful friends who understood the magnitude of the loss. Some of the volunteers I had rescued cats with through the WLPA and I had an elegant afternoon tea party in honour of Lilac and Gardenia and we planted roses in their memory.

I had long had the habit when meditating of sending love to my mother, especially on Mother's Day and her birthday. I would thank her for taking such good care of me. Somehow that had always kept the connection between us open. I began to do the same thing for Gardenia and Lilac, expressing my gratitude for the loving companionship they had given me. Then funny little synchronicities stared happening. Whenever I needed encouragement or confidence something shiny would appear: a sequin or a diamante in the most unlikely place; a metallic lilac Fiat 500 passing me in the fast lane; a glittery card in the mail. More than once, I'd look in the mirror and there would be a piece of glitter on my cheek or chest and I had no idea where it had come from. It was even funnier when the glitter appeared on the face of an unlikely candidate: a helpful bank clerk, a kind stranger, or someone who was going to turn out to be a wonderful new friend.

On my birthday a year after Gardenia and Lilac's passing, I was feeling particularly sad. I sat down at the piano and opened a piece of music I hadn't played in years. I must have placed a card with glitter on it between the pages as a bookmark years before and forgotten about it. The glue had disintegrated. When I opened the music, a mass of glitter fluttered out of it and covered me from head to toe in sparkles. Some people will say that was a sign, others will say it was pure coincidence, or wishful thinking born of grief. But when magic happens, you just know it, don't you?

Emily Brontë

ENGLISH WRITER AND POET (1818–1848)

Emily Brontë wrote *Wuthering Heights* with her cat, Tiger, sleeping near her feet. She shared a love of felines with her sisters, Charlotte and Anne. In her essay, 'The Cat', Brontë argued that cats are not cold and selfish, as many people believe. She claimed that cats differ from other animals in that they are very much like human beings: rather than tear something out of its master's hand, a cat will rub its 'pretty head' against him and reach out its 'velvet paw'. She thought this was comparable to the politeness of human beings, who artfully use their charms to gain what they want.

From feral to fabulous

One Easter I was driving home in the early hours of the morning from an evening out with friends when I passed my local supermarket. The underground car park was lit by fluorescent lights and I saw something out of the corner of my eye. I was sure I had seen a fluffy kitten, too young to be out on its own. I turned my car around and drove into the car park to investigate. Peering out from under a row of shopping trolleys was not one kitten but several. They came out and sat down, their eyes never moving from me. At the front of them, acting like their self-appointed leader, was the fluffy bicolour kitten I'd seen. Her long white coat was patched with light grey and tufts of fur sprouted from the tips of her ears.

The kittens seemed to want something of me. I moved closer and they scattered like marbles. That was when I noticed other watchful eyes on me: two larger cats, a tabby and a tortoiseshell. Where had these cats come from? It was chilly in the car park and I thought of my own cats, Gardenia and Lilac, snuggled on a heated bed at home. My heart was moved by this little family of felines, so I went home, collected some cat food and

Cat wisdom

Willow

*'Make your wishes known. You can't
expect people to guess!'*

✳ ✳ ✳

paper plates and returned to the car park. There was no sign of the kittens or the two adult cats but another female cat with a ruff of fur around her neck, like a lion's mane, was sitting in the car park on her own. She was frightened of me and hid, but when I put the food out she gingerly came out and gobbled it as if she hadn't eaten in weeks.

I've always been a late-night shopper. I hate crowds. I don't like competing over broccoli and beets in the fruit and vegetable department or someone breathing down my neck when I'm trying to decide between 'geranium and lily' or 'orange poppy and lavender' hand soap. I was often at my local supermarket sometime after eleven o'clock at night, usually after an evening out or a dance class, which meant I was overdressed in sequins and high heels—unlike the other shoppers who took late-night shopping in a more relaxed stride: velour tracksuits, shorts without shirts, or even pyjamas and slippers. I also got to know the night-fill staff well, one in particular: Tracey and I struck up a friendship in the toiletries department, where we would share animated conversations about what we were reading. She liked Dean Koontz. I was heavily into Daphne du Maurier and Charles Dickens. We'd also had a cat adventure several years before when I had spotted a tiny kitten living in a drain near the supermarket. Tracey caught her and the kitten was adopted into the loving home of a friend of mine. Little did I know then that we had been practising for cat rescue on a larger scale.

'Have you seen all those cats in the car park?' I asked, the next time I saw Tracey.

She told me she had. In fact, she had been feeding them during the week but she couldn't over the weekends because she lived too far away. Now I understood why I had seen the cats for the first time that Easter weekend: they were hungry. Tracey told me that one of the female cats had been there on her own for some time, but one of the others was dumped and she'd had two female offspring of her own. The kittens I'd seen were the combined litters of the two daughters.

My mind ticked over. Obviously there was an undesexed tomcat around who was impregnating the females. Cats breed rapidly and are like compound interest: their numbers increase exponentially each year. If we didn't do something about getting these cats desexed, there was a possibility that there could be dozens of kittens born in the car park within the next year. Tracey was already spending a fair amount of her pay on feeding the cats that were there, but she wouldn't be able to keep that up for a colony of cats. Then she informed me of an even worse possible outcome.

'Centre Management are getting complaints about the cats. They say they are going to get a pest controller to catch them. I managed to grab the tamest of the kittens and take him home. But I can't take all the others. One of the mother cats and a kitten have already disappeared. I'm worried they have come to some harm.'

In my experience, pest controllers are usually bad news when it comes to anything larger than fleas and termites. I discovered that in my wildlife work with possums. There are protocols that they are supposed to follow regarding native wildlife, but not all do. Tracey had three cats of her own already and a husband whose patience could only be stretched so far. It was apt that she'd named the kitten she'd caught 'Lucky'. If people were already complaining about such a small group of animals, what would happen if there were suddenly a hundred? Anyone who does animal rescue knows that there is a segment of the population that can be chillingly cruel. My fears were confirmed a couple of days later when Tracey told me that a hoon had tried to run over the kittens. We had to get them out of there.

While Tracey fed the cats during the week, I fed them on the weekends. I had no idea how to catch cats that were so unsocialised. We had to get them to trust us while maintaining their wariness of other people who might harm them. Feeding them at a set time and getting them to recognise us seemed the best start. The cats were clever and soon learned to identify our cars when we showed up.

I rang several cat charities, but they all said they couldn't help me. I now understand why. They are inundated with surrendered domestic cats: those acquired as kittens as a novelty Christmas present, no longer wanted now they were grown; the dozens of kittens that resulted from misguided owners who thought they were somehow doing the cat world a favour by letting their female cat have one litter before they desexed her; cats whose owners had died and hadn't made any provision for their feline companions. The charities simply did not have the funds or the volunteers available to trap stray cats.

I searched the internet for what could be done. I came across videos—mainly from the United States—on trap-neuter-and-return programs. The cats were humanely trapped at night, taken to a vet in the morning and desexed, then returned to where they were found. The volunteers would then set up a feeding schedule. It meant that cat colony populations could be kept low and eventually dwindle over time as the cats weren't breeding. This was something, but it wasn't ideal. Desexed or not, the cats in the car park were not safe where they were.

The house I was living in at that time had a workshop attached to it. It didn't have much in it except some gardening tools. It was insulated with sealed windows. It would be a better place to keep the cats until I could find them homes. The idea of finding homes for unsocialised cats was not something promoted on the online videos. There was nobody I spoke to at any of the cat charities who thought trying to find the cats homes was a feasible idea. They were simply too wild for domestic life. Someone suggested a farmer might take them and keep them in a shed, but I didn't think that was a good idea in terms of the local wildlife.

After months of inquiries I had gotten nowhere. The kittens were turning into juveniles. They'd be sexually mature soon and would start breeding with each other. Then I finally found the breakthrough I was looking for: a wonderful woman named Glyn from the Animal Welfare League sent me some discount vouchers to get all the cats desexed and the name of a vet who would be willing to do the procedure. She also warned me that I was very unlikely to be able to socialise the cats, especially the older ones, let alone find them homes. 'You don't know what you are up against,' she warned me. When she realised I was determined she sighed and said, 'Call Halina Thompson at the World League for Protection of Animals. She'll help you.'

Halina arrived the following afternoon. She was petite—five-foot-nothing—of Polish–Ukrainian descent, and a powerhouse of efficiency. She rolled up the sleeves of her cashmere sweater and brushed her hand through her pixie-cut grey hair. 'Right, show me where you intend to put these cats,' she said. She was a perfumed steamroller.

I showed her the workshop and she nodded her approval, all the time eyeing me up and down, assessing if I was the real thing and not some sort of nutter. I explained to her that I was a wildlife volunteer and that I'd humanely trapped possums on many occasions. 'Well, this will be different,' she said, her blue eyes piercing, but her smile impish. 'You trap possums with the idea of treating them then letting them go back to the wild. You are going to be taking these cats out of the wild and then making them fit for a domestic environment. Once you bring them here, you have responsibility for them. If you can't find them homes, they are yours, for the rest of their lives.'

I had a sense then that this was going to be a mammoth undertaking, but at least Halina and I were on the same page. We returned to her car and she took out two metal folded cages. They came up to the top of her head. 'Here, let me help you,' I said, but if I thought my superior height was going to give me superior strength I was wrong. Halina carried her cage towards the workshop as if it was as light as cardboard, while I limped after her, having to stop every so often to put my heavy burden down and rest my arms before picking it up again.

She showed me how to set up a hospital cage for the cats for when they came back from the veterinarian after desexing, with a carry case for a bed that would give them a sense of security, a litter box and food dishes that were fixed to the sides of the cage. There was only enough room to trap two cats at a time and two traps was all I had. I couldn't put any of the cats in my house because one of my own cats, Lilac, had a severe form of inflammatory bowel disease and was on immunosuppressant medication. She couldn't be vaccinated and I couldn't risk her coming into contact with any disease. Even a flea infestation would be serious for her. It was clear that I was going to have to find people to help me, people willing to take the cats and socialise them while I worked on trapping and desexing them. But how to find such people? Most of my social network already had cat companions of their own, didn't have the space, or were already inundated with wildlife in care.

Still, I had committed myself to this course of action so I would simply have to find a way. As a writer, one of the best resources has always been my local library. I started emailing all the librarians I knew to see if anyone could help me. Booklovers and cats were a logical combination. Everyone was sympathetic, but they didn't know anyone who could help. Then Erica, the librarian at Baulkham Hills Library, posted my request on the internal council newsletter and, to my surprise, a woman named Beverley answered me. 'I think I can assist you,' she wrote. 'Give me a call.'

Beverley's warmth radiated from her when she opened her front door and welcomed me into her beautiful home. It was a stunning combination of nouveau country style along with Beverley's own decorative artwork. Beverley was in her late fifties, fabulously groomed and ready to help. Her cat, Marcel, had his own outdoor enclosure complete with a tunnel and landscaped garden. 'But he can let the rescued cats have it for a couple of months,' she offered, generously. I had my beginning. I could trap two cats straight away and bring them to Beverley, who was obviously smart enough and experienced enough with cats of her own to help socialise them. Then I'd be free to trap another two to bring them back to my workshop. It was a slow start, but a start was all I needed.

At eleven o'clock the following Sunday night, Halina and I met in the supermarket car park. It was a freezing winter's night, and dressed in coats, hats and scarves we must have looked like a couple of covert drug dealers. But instead of cocaine, we were dealing in felines.

'I've never met a writer before,' Halina said, jumping from foot to foot and rubbing her arms to keep her circulation going.

'That's because we are usually tucked up at home writing,' I told her, 'not out in a chilly car park late at night trapping cats.'

....

A cat may looke on a kyng, and what of that.
Proverb (mid-sixteenth century)

We set up the traps, which were long metal cages with a trip plate. The idea was to place sardines at the end of the trap: when the cat entered to get the food, it would step on the trip plate and the door of the trap would close behind it. This would be a terrifying experience for the cat, to find itself trapped, and Halina emphasised that we would have to run and cover the cage as soon as possible to calm the animal. It is a cruel thing to set a trap and leave the animal exposed in it overnight. I had seen many pest controllers do that to possums.

The traps set, Halina and I hid around the corner and waited.

'We'll catch the male cats first,' Halina predicted. 'The females are harder to entice. They are more wary and not as food orientated.'

Clang! I jumped. *Clang!* Both traps had shut at the same time, within a matter of minutes.

Halina and I rushed around the corner to find one black male juvenile and his brother, a black-and-white cat, in the traps. She had been right about the boy cats. Their eyes were like saucers and they were banging themselves against the bars, trying to get out. We quickly covered them and checked that the latches on the traps were all secure. If a cat escapes from a trap, you are unlikely to be able to trap them again; they will be forever trap shy. We loaded them into the back of my car, then transferred them to my workshop, where I had installed an oil heater to keep them warm and as calm as possible overnight.

They would have to be transported to the veterinary surgery in their traps first thing the following morning.

The veterinarian recommended by the Animal Welfare League was on the outskirts of Sydney, in a rural belt. Suburban veterinarians are usually not willing to risk their fingers with unsocialised cats. I waited in the reception area with the two cats in the covered traps while the receptionist dealt with people who had come in with sick chickens, a pet piglet and a border collie with a thorn in his foot. As I waited, volunteers from other charities arrived, one with no less than three crates of puppies and a similar amount of kittens. It was a visual clue to the tragedy of people not getting their animals desexed.

I already knew from the WLPA literature Halina had given me that a quarter of a million healthy cats and dogs are destroyed in Australian pounds each year simply because there are not enough homes for them. That number did not include all the animals that were euthanised humanely in shelters and at private veterinary surgeries, or the animals drowned, shot, poisoned or dumped, as the female cat in my local supermarket car park had been. Irresponsible owners, puppy mills and people acquiring animals from pet stores instead of shelters or pounds were all exacerbating the problem. Mahatma Gandhi once said that the greatness of a nation and its moral progress could be judged by how it treats animals. By those standards, Australia was doing poorly. In keeping with their greater populations, Britain and the United States have even larger numbers of 'death-row pets'.

I returned later that day to pick up the two cats after their operations. While they were still groggy from the anaesthetic, they had been transferred to cat carriers. As well as being desexed, they had been vaccinated and microchipped. The receptionist, a prim woman with stiff hair and an even stiffer smile, handed me the registration form. The cats' names had already been filled in as 'WLPA 1 black male' and 'WLPA 2 black & white male'.

'Oh no,' I told her, 'I'm going to give them proper names.'

The receptionist cocked her eyebrow. 'What are you going to call them? They are feral cats, not pets.'

I sensed the other people in the waiting room were listening to our conversation, curious to hear what I might answer. They were good country folk, in faded jeans and old sweaters with holes in the elbows. People who cared enough about their working dogs and barnyard pets to take them to the vet, but not the kind of people who would stand for too much nonsense. I glanced at the sleepy-eyed cats I had rescued. They were handsome, sleek and panther-like, despite the living conditions they had been born into. I had ambitions for them. They deserved grand names: names they could aspire to. I'd been to an Italian wedding a few weeks before where everyone had been decked out in designer clothes, topped off with fabulously big hair and gold-coloured acrylic nails. It had been lavish and over the top, from the hanging floral centrepieces and the luxe nine-layer cake, to the smoke machine that had pumped out a fog of fantasy onto the dance floor for the bridal waltz and the cannon that had shot out rose petals.

I took a breath and met the receptionist's gaze. 'Valentino and Versace,' I told her. 'Those are their names.'

You could have heard a pin drop.

Halina had to hold her belly to stop herself laughing when I told her what I'd named the cats. 'Who on earth is going to own a couple of cats named Valentino and Versace?' She asked. 'Can you imagine someone standing in their backyard calling out: "Valentino! Versace!"'

I didn't know it then, but there would be someone exactly suited to having a couple of cats named Valentino and Versace. But in the meantime the pair were to have a cameo appearance in *Sapphire Skies* as the cats of Doctor Luka Demidov.

Lily frowned. 'I don't understand what you mean. He's gay ... isn't he?

Oksana stared at her as if she'd just confessed she was an alien from outer space. 'Where did you get that idea?'

Lily shifted uneasily. Where had she got the idea? 'He's cute, he dresses well, he can cook, he likes to dance ... he has cats named Valentino and Versace.'

Zsa Zsa and Eva Gabor

HUNGARIAN-AMERICAN ACTRESSES
(ZSA ZSA, 1917-2016; EVA, 1919-1995)

Zsa Zsa Gabor was known for her glamorous appearance and her extravagant lifestyle, and she also understood the value of feline friendship. Many times married, she is reported to have said, 'My husband said it was him or the cat. I miss him sometimes.' Her equally glamorous sister, Eva, was the voice of Duchess in the charming Disney animated romantic comedy, *The Aristocats* (1970). In a plot that doesn't sound implausible, Madame Adelaide Bonfamille, a retired opera diva, wishes to leave her fortune to her cat, Duchess, and her three kittens; however, Bonfamille's evil butler, Edgar, plots to get rid of the cats and claim the inheritance for himself. He dumps the cats in the countryside, where an alley cat aptly named Thomas offers to help Duchess and her kittens return to Paris. Of course, romance is in the air for the unlikely couple. Ahhh!

After Valentino and Versace went off to be cared for by Beverley, Halina and I were ready to go trapping again. It took us two attempts to catch the bicolour cat I'd first seen, who I named Lou Lou (after the perfume), then Sophie (after the Countess of Wessex) and Gucci (the younger half-brother of Valentino and Versace). Each time the receptionist had to fill in the names on a registration form I could feel her despise me more and more. Things almost came to a head between us with Gucci; and I had to admit he was a little problematic.

After being caught and desexed, the previous cats had gone quiet and kept themselves low in their cat carriers. Cats are not only predators, but they are also prey for larger animals. It's a defence mechanism for them to make themselves as quiet and as invisible as possible. Gucci did not follow this pattern. He went into full-blown attack. When I took him in his trap to the veterinary surgery, he was punching his paw through the gaps in the wire and growling, hissing and spitting. When he was placed in the hospital room with the other domestic cats to await his operation, he set them all off yowling. The atmosphere in the surgery became the soundtrack to a creepy Vincent Price film. Gucci had been caught in what's called a 'crush trap'. It sounds awful, but what it means is that the door of the trap can be moved forward so that the animal is forced to the back to the cage. Getting the cat into a tight space where it can't turn makes it easier to jab it with a sedative injection so that the veterinarian can then properly administer the anaesthetic for the operation. Despite the design of the trap, and Gucci being given a sedative, it still took three vet nurses to hold him down with a pillow so the vet could give him the anaesthetic. He was the smallest of the male cats but the feistiest. Even when I picked him up later that day, still groggy from the anaesthetic, he was growling and hissing. Because he was completely black, when I peered into the carry cage all I could see were his white fang-like teeth and his golden eyes. He truly was a 'devil cat'.

'That one will never come good,' the veterinarian advised me. 'He's third generation feral and already nine months old. It would probably have been better if you'd had him euthanised. I guess you are just going to let him go where you found him.'

The receptionist nodded her agreement.

'Oh no,' I told them. 'I will find Gucci a home . . . and incidentally the World League doesn't refer to cats like him as "feral". He simply hasn't been properly socialised yet.'

The veterinarian shook his head as if I was insane. I slinked out of the surgery with the devil incarnate snarling and hissing at everyone in the waiting room as we went.

Sophie, the grandma of the colony, was the tamest of the cats. It was obvious that she had once been someone's pet before she'd been dumped at the supermarket. Although she was initially nervous, she took to being cared for easily and she seemed faintly bemused by Gucci's antics as he spat and hissed at me whenever I tried to put food in the hospital cage or change the kitty litter. I had to hold a stick and a piece of board between us like some sort of Victorian circus lion tamer. But after a few days, Gucci's personality changed. Part of it may have been that his hormones settled, although he was still young, but part of it was, I think, his own realisation: 'I'm warm, I'm being fed, this lady isn't hurting me, there is soft classical music being played on the radio and my grandmother doesn't seem at all perturbed . . . what am I fighting for?' Suddenly he went from trying to kill me to looking at me with adoring eyes, and rubbing against me and even accepting being cuddled and held!

My spiritual sister Melinda and I often remind each other of Gucci's incredible transformation when we are going through challenges ourselves. The night Halina and I trapped Sophie and Gucci had been bitterly cold. As I waited for Halina to arrive, I'd watched Sophie and Gucci climb in and out of rubbish bins looking for food. We hadn't fed the cats the day before catching them, so that hunger would entice them to take the food in the traps. My heart bled for them and my whole intention for Sophie and Gucci was to get them out of a dangerous situation and into a better life. But from Gucci's perspective, once he was in the trap and put into a car and driven away from the home he'd known since his birth, he must have thought he was going to die. It would have been a terrifying experience for him. Now, safe in his forever home, he never has to worry about hunger and no longer suffers the discomfort of worms and fleas. He will also have a much longer life span now that he isn't exposed to disease and doesn't have to risk his eyes and limbs to fight for territory. It should be added that he also is cherished by his human 'cat-mother', sits on her lap and cuddles up to her when she is reading in bed, stars in her Instagram account, and is even included in a trust fund should anything happen to her. He has truly travelled from feral to fabulous.

The point that Melinda and I make to each other is that sometimes when something seemingly horrible happens to us, the worst thing we could imagine, the Divine has a bigger plan for us that we can't see yet; perhaps to take us out of an unsatisfactory, or even dangerous, situation and place us somewhere far better. But often we fight tooth and nail for the status quo simply because we can't envision the bigger picture. When Melinda and I recall Gucci's story, we remind each other not to panic, but to allow ourselves to go with the flow of life with a sense of trust.

I already had Lou Lou, Sophie and Gucci in my workshop and to make room for the remaining cats I had to find them homes as soon as I could. I had been corresponding via email with a lovely woman named Gloria who had lost her pet cockatiel. I had found one, but sadly it didn't turn out to be hers. Yet we'd kept up a friendly correspondence. By chance

Cat wisdom

Smokey

'There is a time for hunting and a time for sleeping ...
and sleeping some more!'

✳ ✳ ✳

I asked her if she was interested in adopting a cat and sent
her a picture of Sophie, who was a beautiful classic tabby cat
with an ochre coat spectacularly marked with black stripes,
dots and swirls. Gloria told me that they had recently lost a
beloved, elderly cat and she was keen to come and see Sophie.
Her husband, Steve, wasn't so sure. But as soon as they both saw
Sophie, and she them, it was love at first sight. Sophie relaxed
into Gloria's embrace as if she knew she would be deeply cared
for by her. Indeed, she went off to a life of luxury in the coastal
suburb of Freshwater where Gloria and Steve lavish her with
love . . . and I get to see pictures of her sleeping on their bed,

gazing out the window at their leafy street and joining in on family occasions.

Lou Lou was still unsettled and needed more time to get used to a domestic life and being handled. That left Gucci, and it was clear that it was a love affair on both sides between us. He would greet me whenever I walked into the workshop with a stretch and a purr, and always wanted to snuggle with me. For my part, I couldn't resist his compact body and those beautiful eyes that watched my every move with intelligence and grace. Still, I had to be careful about Lilac, so before I could commit to adding him to my household, I had to make sure he wasn't carrying any diseases. I would have to take him to Marilyn, my local veterinarian.

Remembering how badly he'd behaved at the surgery where he'd been desexed, the idea filled me with dread. So we prepared for the day with all the care of a coach training an athlete. The first hurdle was to get him used to sitting in his carrier while I carted him to and from the car, then once we had conquered that I added a short practice drive around the block. After doing that for a week, I drove further and further each time until we eventually reached the veterinary surgery car park before turning home again. Once back in the workshop I would feed him a treat and brush him, something he had grown to love, so he would associate the trip as culminating with an enjoyable reward.

After a few weeks, we were ready for the big day. The training paid off. Gucci was relaxed in the car and watched the scenery whiz by with a nonchalant air.

'Gucci,' I said to him, 'I would love you to come and live with me, but to do that you have to behave at this appointment. Please do not bite or scratch anyone.'

He looked at me with those old soul eyes of his. Was it possible that he had understood what I'd asked of him?

Having been warned that I was bringing an unsocialised cat, Marilyn had made an appointment for the quietest time of the day. But when Gucci and I arrived in the waiting room, it seemed that every man and his dog, literally, were there. I don't know if there was something in the atmosphere that day, but there was a line-up of canines with thorns in their paws, stomach upsets and sudden-onset skin rashes. Although I had covered Gucci's carrier with a towel, I could feel him moving nervously inside it. He jumped when an overly curious labrador put his nose up to the carrier. I couldn't have imagined a worse scenario for setting off his terror again.

Marilyn ushered us into the examination room and I placed Gucci's carrier on the examination table. She had a Swedish student vet with her and she turned to her, saying sagely, 'And this is the feral cat I was telling you about. We must handle him with caution.' She eased off the cover to reveal Gucci. He sat blinking at her like a regal prince.

'Mrrh, prrh,' he greeted the vets, in a friendly cat language.

He didn't even wriggle as I took him out of the carrier and placed him on his blanket on the examination table. Then he rolled over from side to side with all the charm of a household moggy lounging in front of the fire.

'Oh, he's so handsome!' exclaimed Marilyn. Gucci blinked at the compliment and rolled over some more.

'I've never seen a cat so calm at the vet,' agreed the student, rubbing him under the chin. 'He can't possibly have come from the wild.'

I was too gobsmacked to say anything.

Gucci's behaviour that day was the most exemplary I had seen from any of my cats. I cringed each time Marilyn put her fingers in his mouth, ears and even in his eye to take swabs. But he took all the prodding and poking with dignified composure. Then when she went to draw blood from his neck vein, I gritted my teeth expecting Gucci to turn into the devil cat again, but he kept his eyes steadily on me the whole time. When the ordeal was over, he slept peacefully in the car on the way home. The results came back a week later. He was in the clear.

Fortunately, because Gardenia and Lilac had always had each other, and Gucci had been surrounded by cats, introducing him to the girls went fairly smoothly. After the initial period of getting Gucci settled into the spare room, I went about familiarising the cats with each other. First by smell: rubbing each of the cats with a clean sock then getting them to sniff each other's scents; swapping their bedding around; using the same brush on all of them; and finally exchanging kitty litter samples. Second by sound: feeding them on either side of a door so they could hear each other. Thirdly by sight: putting them in their cat carriers and gradually, over days, moving the cat carriers closer together. And finally, by sleep: I would put them in their cat carriers then take a nap right in front of them. They would eventually all fall asleep too. It's my theory that napping together is the ultimate act of trust between cats—and humans!

When it came time for the cats to mingle together, none of the cats was particularly fazed, but it certainly helped that Gardenia was such a diva. Whenever she deemed Gucci was getting out of hand, she would put her paw on his forehead and he would then throw himself on the floor submissively. If ever he tried to assert territory at the top of the cat tower she would simply nudge him off to the bottom rung. She certainly knew how to put him in his place and I think, like everybody else, he was a little in awe of her.

What surprised me most was what Gardenia and Lilac, the super-privileged of the cat elite, taught Gucci:

♥ 'The best seat in the house is always yours for the taking.'

♥ 'If cat-mother isn't up early enough to feed you breakfast at an hour pleasing to you, it's quite proper to climb all over her, pat her face with your paw and meow loudly directly into her ear. If that doesn't work, take a running leap and jump onto her with your full weight!'

♥ 'Nothing deserves cat-mother's attention as much as you. If she spends too long on the telephone, nip her leg.'

♥ 'If you don't like the food you are presented with, turn your nose away from it or pretend to bury it. Do this a few times until something better is presented to you.' (And this behaviour from a cat who used to find his food in the rubbish bin!)

Gucci taught Gardenia and Lilac a thing or two as well. His most impressive display was to 'kill' the door draught stoppers, which he obviously thought were snakes. He would warn Gardenia and Lilac away from the 'dangerous beasts', then seize the draught stoppers by 'the throat' and shake them until they were dead. Then, with the floor covered in sand and the draught stopper 'deceased', Gucci would turn to Gardenia and Lilac as if to say, 'There, it's safe to walk by now.'

Gardenia and Lilac always snuggled up with each other when they slept. Gucci clearly longed to join them. He would wait until they were asleep and then gradually inch himself closer to them until his rump was touching theirs. Then he would try overlapping a paw or resting a head on one or the other's back. Gardenia would open one eye and he'd inch away, only to try again later. Then one day I came home and found all three of them snuggled together; from that time on, they were great friends.

Like Sophie, Rosie—the beautiful female cat with the ruff—appeared to have once been a pet. The fact that she never had a litter of kittens indicated that she had probably been desexed. Thankfully, she was so attached to Tracey, who had named her before I got in with one of my auspicious appellations, that she didn't need to be trapped. Tracey was able to put her in a cat carrier and Beverley decided to adopt her as a companion to Marcel. With Valentino and Versace in Beverley's enclosure, and Sophie, Gucci and Rosie in their forever homes, it now came down to capturing the elusive tortoiseshell, Rainbow: Valentino, Versace and Lou Lou's mother and Sophie's daughter.

Halina was right that female cats could be particularly difficult to trap, but we had more troubles than that. While Gucci had been cantankerous when we caught him, Rainbow was downright ferocious. While the others had accepted food from us, Rainbow never had. She watched us with suspicion and fear. Who could blame her? We suspect that her sister and one of her sister's kittens (the sibling of Gucci and Lucky) had met an unpleasant end at the hands of a local cat hater. Having failed to tempt her into a normal trap on several occasions, we decided to use a much larger and more complicated trap called a box trap, which would involve enticing Rainbow to food in a certain area then pulling a piece of rope to bring the larger trap down on her.

It was already August and there was someone's undesexed pet tomcat—that we had nicknamed Casanova—hanging around. It's not uncommon for owners of male cats to not get their cats desexed, figuring the litters of kittens that will result over the years are not their problem. But this sort of lack of responsibility is one of the contributing reasons to why staggering numbers of kittens are being euthanised in pounds and shelters each year. They also don't realise that there are a number of benefits to getting a male cat desexed for both themselves and the animal: a desexed male will not be aggressive or spray for territory; he will roam less, which means he is less likely to be hit by a car, killed by a dog or end up with fight wounds; and desexing a male cat helps prevent prostate and other cancers.

As the situation regarding Rainbow was getting desperate, I went to the cemetery to ask for my mother's help. It had been raining during the day, but the afternoon sun began to shine as I stood before my mother's tombstone.

'Mum,' I prayed, 'if we don't get Rainbow tonight and she has kittens it's going to be very difficult to find them all homes. Please help us.'

I raised my eyes and a smile came to my face. A deep sense of peace enveloped me. There, stretched across the sky and arching over the Rookwood Necropolis, was a rainbow.

I paused a moment to drink in the stripes of red, orange, yellow and violet. My mother and cats have always been a mystical combination.

That night, Halina and I set up the box trap then hid in the bushes, preparing ourselves for a long night. Then we heard a *clang!* Rainbow had not approached the box trap but had entered one of the standard traps we had also laid out as a backup. When we ran to the trap to cover it we had to peer in it several times to make sure the cat we had caught was indeed Rainbow, and not somebody's pet. After weeks of trying to trap her, the whole process had taken less than ten minutes.

We may have finally trapped Rainbow, but getting her to settle down in the presence of humans was a different matter. On her first night in her hospital cage she turned everything in it upside down and shredded her bedding. I walked into the workshop the following morning to be greeted by tufts of polyester fibre floating in the air. Lou Lou, who was now out of a cage and free to walk around the workshop, looked perturbed. When I went to tidy Rainbow's water and food dishes she lashed out at me with an almighty snarl, and I moved my hand just in time to avoid serious injury. I had never seen a cat like her. She was far worse than Gucci had been. When she remained for a week like that, I began to think keeping her was cruel. Halina came to assess the situation and even she looked worried. We decided to keep Rainbow until we were sure she was completely healed from her operation and didn't show any sign of infection, then we would have to decide what to do. I found dealing with her food and litter tray each day stressful. I had to arm myself with gloves, a board and a stick and protective goggles. I was more like someone dealing with a wild lion than a stray cat. Still, I thought of that afternoon at the cemetery and the peace I had felt and something told me to persist.

Fortunately, Lou Lou was making fast progress now and turning into a really lovely cat. She loved being brushed and I had gotten her used to being cuddled. I'd had to do it in stages, first getting her used to the pressure of my hands on her sides then gradually lifting her an inch or two higher off the ground each day. It took about a month, but I could now cuddle her and when I pressed her to my chest she would nudge my chin with her own. Rainbow used to watch our interaction with her face scrunched up into a frown and growl. I decided to win her over by diffusing any sense of threat she felt from me.

I was able to place her in a larger enclosure in the workshop so she had plenty of room to move around. I would take my laptop down to the workshop and spend the day writing there, letting her watch me and not paying her any attention other than to occasionally look up at her and say her name softly and gently. If you want to win over a cat, you need to let them observe you and let them approach you. It took nearly two months, but gradually Rainbow started coming out of her carry case and observing me more closely.

Mark Twain

AMERICAN WRITER AND HUMOURIST
(1835–1910)

Mark Twain made no secret that he liked cats better than people. 'If man could be crossed with a cat, it would improve man, but it would deteriorate the cat.' Twain owned multiple cats at a time, but he kept track of them all by giving them illustrious names such as Beelzebub, Buffalo Bill or Zoroaster. When Twain travelled, he would rent cats to keep him company. After returning the cats to their owners he would leave money behind to cover their care for their lifetimes. When his cat Bambino went missing, Twain penned a superb 'Lost Cat' notice: 'Large and intensely black; thick, velvety fur; has a faint fringe of white hair across his chest; not easy to find in ordinary light.' Fortunately, Bambino found his own way home.

I placed a new long-handled paintbrush in her cage and let her sniff it, then I used it to softly brush her under the chin and around her cheeks. She enjoyed being touched that way and would purr. Still she was wary of me if I got too close, and believe me, I was wary of her. A long-handled paintbrush was as close as I was going to allow my fingers anywhere near those sharp teeth of hers.

When I wasn't in the workshop, I would leave the radio on ABC Classic FM. Not just for the music but for the soft, well-articulated tones of the announcers. I wanted Rainbow and Lou Lou to get used to different human voices. Gradually I also introduced them to the sounds of household appliances: the rumble of a kettle boiling, the murmur of the television, or the high-pitched hum of a hairdryer. This Finishing School for Stray Cats went on for another couple of months. Then one day as I was cleaning Rainbow's enclosure, she reached out her paw from her carry case (where she usually hid when I was tidying up).

'Mrrh! Prrh!' she greeted me, stretching her paw out closer towards me.

I glanced at her long, untrimmed claws. I sensed that she wanted me to reach out too, but I was worried that if I did and she turned on me, that would be the end of piano playing for me. Still, it seemed like a friendly gesture. I reached out my hand and touched her paw. Then she rolled over. I looked at her face and the frown she always wore had disappeared from it. Her expression was relaxed and soft and I finally got to see how beautiful she was. Her chin, chest and front legs were pure white and the tortoiseshell markings on her face were beautiful. Her ears and aqua eyes were masked in black while her forehead and nose were caramel, as was one of her cheeks. It was a beautiful moment of trust and I realised how far Rainbow and I had come, and how incredible change is possible. I had never expected Rainbow to turn around quite like this.

To complete Finishing School for Lou Lou and Rainbow, I had everyone and anyone who came to the house visit them too. I had to get them used to as many different types of people and their smells as possible. Valentino and Versace had been in Beverley's enclosure for much longer than the initially agreed two months. Although she was very generous about it, I had to find the homes for the remaining cats. Lou Lou and Rainbow had grown dear to me and I wanted the right people for them. As it turned out, Halina found them for me. In the supermarket one day a woman remarked to her that she was buying a lot of cat food, they got talking and the woman mentioned to Halina that her daughter wanted a tortoiseshell cat!

Julie came to see Rainbow with her two young children, Hannah and Matthew. It was obvious from the moment I met them that there was something special about this family. Hannah and Matthew were gentle with the cats, waiting for Lou Lou and Rainbow to approach them rather than forcing themselves on the cats as children—and adults—often do. Julie told me that the family had recently adopted an elderly golden retriever, Oscar, who had been surrendered to a shelter. This is a common scenario I hear about from my friends who are involved in canine rescue: elderly dogs, no longer active and requiring too much care, are handed over to shelters and even pounds. It seems so heartless to abandon a faithful companion simply because they are old, but that's what people do. Julie and her family had gone to the shelter with the intention of adopting a puppy, and had come home with gentle Oscar.

I hoped Julie would take Lou Lou as well as Rainbow because the mother and daughter seemed to give each other confidence. I was thrilled when they agreed. Hannah and Matthew had two older siblings and Julie's husband was also good with animals, so Lou Lou and Rainbow couldn't have gone to a better home. They took a while to settle into their new environment, but before long Lou Lou was sleeping on Hannah's bed and Rainbow became Julie's special companion, following her around during the day as she went about her tasks.

Beverley brought Valentino and Versace to me and I set them up in the workshop. Despite all my endeavours, I hadn't been able to find them homes. They had been together for so long that I didn't want to separate them, but it was next to impossible to find someone who wanted two eighteen-month-old black boy cats. But truth be told, I think their destiny was always to end up with me. After all, I had named their younger half-brother Gucci. Valentino, Versace and Gucci has a kind of ring to it, I think! Gardenia and Lilac had both been diagnosed with terminal illnesses by then, and I didn't want to introduce two bigger cats to them when they were growing frail, but I knew that one day Gucci would be alone and that he would miss Lilac and Gardenia. So I made the workshop into a homely space and installed a cat enclosure on the outside of it so Valentino and Versace could climb out the window into it and sit in the sunshine. When Lilac and then Gardenia passed away, I waited for the worst of my grief to soften before reuniting Valentino, Versace and Gucci together in my house, and the little trio has done everything together since.

The years have passed by quickly, and as I write this, the three boy cats, all in sparkly diamante collars, are fast asleep on the sofa next to me. In the past year, I have suffered a series of traumatic events and have passed many dark nights of the soul when I wondered if life could ever feel good or safe again. But when I look at my three blissfully peaceful cats, I think of the incredible journey they made from wild kittens born in a car park to beloved companions, and I realise that miraculous transformations are always possible. All things can be healed with love, time and trust in life. I reach forward and pat each of their silky heads and they purr in response. They are my inspiration. As they travelled from feral to fabulous, so too must I set my course for a positive life adventure ahead.

3

The fairy cat-mothers

One of the wonderful aspects of volunteering to help animals has been the friends I've made along the way. I get together with the women who helped me rescue the cats from the supermarket car park, either by adopting or fostering the cats or helping find adopters, a couple of times year for lunch. We call those occasions 'The Cat Ladies' Lunch' and celebrate not only our love of cats, but also the warm bonds of friendship formed as a result of that rescue. Tracey, Julie and her daughter Hannah, Beverley, Helen, Clare, Gloria, Halina and I are all from such different walks of life that we may not have crossed paths with each other any other way. What I love most about these women is their innate kindness. They took on the care of animals that were frightened, shunned and unwanted and gave them lives they would never have otherwise had. And those animals transformed with their love.

Halina, especially, has become a mentor to me, exactly the kind of woman I admire. She is strong yet gentle, determined but wise enough to know when to stand back and take direction from her intuition. She is kind, but she won't stand for fools—and cruel people had better get out of her way because she might be tiny, but she will take them out one way or another! Halina's compassionate speech builds up cats and people, but a sharp word from her can leave the biggest bully trembling in his or her shoes. We connect on so many levels, but what I treasure most is her vast life experience. I think of all of this as I drive through the semirural district in Sydney's north-west where Halina lives.

I pull up at the gate and sense dozens of pairs of eyes watching me. There are flashes of fur and tails disappearing into the mulberry bushes that line the driveway when I alight from the car. It is spring and a warm, balmy breeze tickles my face, bringing with it the scent of jasmine and freshly mown grass. I have a sense of entering an enchanted world where I am being watched by fairies. Indeed, as I stop and look around I realise there are cats everywhere: asleep under trees, next to statues, on cushions on the balcony. They appear from bushes, from rooftops, from behind wheelbarrows and hedges. Halina has fifty of them all together. But these are not your usual cats.

At the WLPA adoption centre in Gladesville, the cats and kittens live in an indoor open-plan arrangement with capsules, platforms and hideaways. Only the kittens are kept enclosed in order to prevent them from getting underfoot. It's painted bright white and attended to by devoted volunteers who answer telephones and otherwise go about their tasks with a cat or two lounging on their desks. These are all the cats that have good prospects for adoption.

The cats at Halina's property don't. They are the truly unwanted. The first time I came to the property there had been a cat flu epidemic in several of the stray-cat colonies around Sydney. This terrible disease can cause eye ulcers, particularly in kittens, that can progress to serious damage and result in the loss of the eye. Halina had rescued a group of young cats and kittens that needed one of their eyes removed to avoid death from a serious infection. I remember looking into one of the rooms of her cattery and seeing a dozen of these one-eyed cats looking up at me as if they were winking. They were now well fed and cared for, but not likely to be adopted except by the most kind-hearted of people. That is the challenge of the WLPA, of which Halina is the tireless president. It is an entirely self-funded, volunteer-run charity with a no-kill policy. They will not put an animal down simply because it is unwanted.

I knock on the front door to the ranch-style home, but there is no answer; well, not a human one, anyway. A dozen sleepy cats look up at me from their beds, then go back to their slumber. I walk around to the back of the house and find Halina busy cleaning rows of litter trays, watched by a group of tortoiseshell and ginger cats. She is wearing slacks and a blouse and apologises to me for her appearance, but to me she looks like some sort of glamorous farmer.

'Come, meet everybody,' she says, guiding me around her sprawling fenced-in garden with its arbours, trellises and hedges. As we walk, she tells me about the cats and something of their history. There's a handsome green-eyed male named Emerald, who is feline immunodeficiency virus (FIV) positive and was left behind by his owner when she moved away, and a gorgeous pure white cat named Blondie who was rescued from a cat colony and is too wary of people to be touched. 'Blondie was living along with a group of cats in the garden of a public housing complex that was about to be demolished,' Halina explains. 'The developer didn't care if there were cats living there or not. He put up a fence around it and locked us out so we couldn't feed them. The bulldozers were about to move in, but a kind security guard let us in and we were able to either get the cats out or move them to another site.'

'What would have happened if the security guard hadn't let you in?' I ask her.

She purses her lips and shakes her head. 'They'd all be dead by now.'

Halina indicates two tortoiseshell cats that came from a hoarding household. 'Hoarders present us with particular difficulties,' she explains. 'They think they are saving the cats, but they trap them in dreadful living conditions. In the place those two girls came from, there was so much filth it was unbelievable. Some of the cats were starving. If one of the cats died, the others would be so hungry they'd eat it.'

Many of the cats in Halina's care have lived by their wits for so long it's too difficult to socialise them to a point where they could be adopted. Others are elderly, abandoned by their owners in old age or too frail to continue to live in colonies. A great number of the cats bear the scars on their faces and bodies of the atrocious conditions from which they came. And yet, they are now living in a cats' paradise and their demeanours show it. Halina knows each of these cats as individuals and, as she talks to them, they respond with relaxed, trusting eyes. There is a loving bond between Halina and the cats, and it touches my heart to see it.

'People wonder how I can live with so many cats with so many different personalities and needs,' Halina tells me, 'but when I was a small child I was sent to boarding school in Belgium. I was one of the youngest of a large group of girls and I learned to get along with everybody, including the nuns, by acknowledging each person as an individual. I had fun with the friendly girls, was gentle with the timid ones and was sympathetic with the grumpy ones. It was all good training for how I live now! You simply learn to adapt.'

Halina invites me to sit down with her on her verandah. She takes an orange and peels it with an enormous chef's knife. Suddenly the air of 'professional businesswoman' she usually exudes dissipates and she turns into a woodswoman, which makes sense because I know that she grew up in rural Germany. Born of a Polish father and Ukrainian mother who had been taken to Germany as forced farm labour during the war, Halina is an interesting mix of life experience. Her accent is a blend of her European origins with sophisticated English inflections and mannerisms picked up from years of living in London.

'I had an idyllic life as a child,' she explains. 'It was a gift to grow up in the woods of Germany. Everything was so magical. My mother had a deep affinity with nature and she passed that on to me. I knew the name of every plant, flower and herb that grew in the forest around us before I even went to school. She told me and my siblings not to climb the lilac trees that grew in the garden because we would break their branches and hurt their spirits.'

Halina's description reminds me of the pagan belief that the Divine expresses itself in every animate being and inanimate object. I wonder if Halina has brought some of that fairy magic to her own garden and that was what I sensed when I arrived. It's a pity that in Australian culture we don't always have the same level of appreciation. We live in one of the most beautiful countries in the world, but I have often seen Australian children picking at the bark of trees until they practically ringbark them, or stomping on ants for the fun of it while their parents simply look on. An acquaintance in the countryside often expresses her frustration that people continue to throw their rubbish out of their car windows, despite years of government advertising that this kills wildlife and can ignite bushfires.

'When did you realise you had a special empathy with animals?' I ask Halina.

'When I went to Belgium,' she answers. 'For the first time I visited homes with canaries in cages and I found the idea of it distressing. Birds should fly freely. Then I heard a pig being slaughtered and the memory of that has stayed with me all these years.'

As Halina talks, something interesting is happening. I look around and notice some of the cats have come to join us. They have gathered around and are lying on their haunches with their eyes closed as my own cats do at home when I have guests or am reading or playing the piano. Cats are far from aloof animals. Even these ones, who have suffered so much at the hands of humans, seem to be enjoying our company. I ask Halina how she first became involved with the WLPA.

'It was back in the late nineties,' she says. 'I joined because of native animals, especially because of the cruel treatment of kangaroos. There was a debate at the time about whether cats and dogs should be banned in Australia and people should only be allowed to keep native animals as pets. I couldn't imagine anything worse. Cats and dogs have been domesticated for thousands of years. Our native animals should remain wild. We need to focus on keeping their habitat, not try and turn them into pets.'

I shudder at the idea too. My own work with wildlife gives me insight about why such a proposal would be a disaster. I know how much care our native animals need. No matter if it was a heatwave or pouring with rain, I would have to go out to collect native plants for the animals in my care to eat. The mammals also can't be house-trained like cats, rabbits and dogs. You won't get a brushtail possum to use a litter box, or an adult bandicoot to sit contentedly on your lap while you watch television. They'd all have to be kept in cages most of the time. If the thousands of dogs, cats and rabbits in Australian pounds are an indication, many human beings aren't capable of being responsible for animals that are relatively easy to maintain—you can buy pet food at the supermarket, after all. So how could they ever be trusted to maintain native animals? Perhaps when the novelty of their 'pet' sugar glider or owl or wombat wore off, they would stick the animal out in the bush as a solution. But a tame animal would not cope with life in the wild and would quickly perish by predation or starvation. If by chance it did survive, its presence would put a strain on those animals already living in that area.

'What about cats?' I ask Halina. 'How did you end up doing so much work with cats?'

Halina smiles. 'I've always had a special affinity with cats. I can't even explain it. One day when I was very young, a neighbour's cat appeared on our doorstep and we looked at each other as if we recognised each other. My connection with cats feels like something ancient, a shared genetic memory perhaps. That's why I feel so committed to their welfare; I sense that I am indebted to them in some way.

'One day, someone brought a cat into the WLPA office that they had rescued from a notoriously bad Sydney pound. The cat was in an awful condition: sick, malnourished, and with matted fur and a weeping skin rash. He was expected to die, but I gradually nursed him back to health. That's when I first became aware of the horror of the conditions at that pound. You could not imagine the terrible enclosures in which the cats and dogs were kept. There was little attempt to find them homes and they were basically waiting there to be euthanised. There was no hope for those animals and anybody going there with the idea of adopting an animal would have been distressed by the conditions.

'I made contact with a wonderful councillor who had a tremendous sense of justice for both people and animals. With his support we formed a group—"Friends of the Pound"—and eventually were able to get volunteers in at the pound to improve the conditions there. It's taken a couple of decades of hard work, but the pound now desexes animals before adopting them out and there is even talk of it becoming a no-kill shelter. There's still a lot of work to be done and a few years ago a rogue councillor wanted to overturn the desexing policy. That shows we can never become complacent: there is always some idiot ready to throw a spanner in the works. But the council is getting to the root cause of the problem of an oversupply of animals and that is incredibly encouraging.'

Halina and I take a moment to reflect on how the idea of owning a 'rescue cat' or a 'pound dog' has become a source of pride, particularly over the past decade. While dog breeds vary widely from the ginormous Saint Bernards to the tiny miniature Chihuahuas, essentially the cat has maintained a similar size and appearance across the breeds. Only occasionally am I asked what breed of cat I have. There is a lot less snobbery around cat breeds than there is with dogs. People don't judge my personality and social status on what type of cat I have.

Gardenia and Lilac were beautiful purebred cream Burmese. They were meant to come into my life at that particular time and I will always be glad they did, but I would be unlikely to obtain a cat from a breeder again. My personal opinion is that the notion that a cat will have a certain personality because of its breeding is highly unlikely. Gardenia and Lilac came from the same top breeder, were siblings from the same litter, and were treated by me with exactly the same love and attention, and yet they turned out to have completely different personalities to each other. They were very friendly cats, something for which Burmese are supposedly known, but I wonder how much more that owed to their environment rather than genetics. Gardenia had no sense of danger, because she'd never been confronted with it. Every person was a good person as far as she was concerned, because no other type of person had ever entered her experience. I also know people with unfriendly Burmese cats that bite them.

Gucci, Valentino and Versace are street cats, born into a dangerous environment. They are all related to each other, but also have completely different personalities. Gucci is highly alert, possessive and smart. Valentino is a puddle of love that could spend all day on my lap, staring into my eyes. Unlike Gucci, who perks up at every sound and is wary of even a new cushion on the sofa, Valentino doesn't concern himself with much and would probably only trouble himself to break into a slow run if the house was on fire. Versace is the quiet, wise observer. He likes to spend his time on windowsills watching the birds and butterflies.

The other thing to consider is health. I loved Lilac with all my heart but her numerous health problems meant she was at the veterinary surgery at least twice a month, even when she was still young. All the vets we saw made the same

Cat wisdom

Biscuit

'You train people how to treat you. Look at how well we cats have trained you!'

✳ ✳ ✳

comment: purebred cats are more prone to genetic diseases, while everyday moggies are stronger because of their mixed breeding. Black cats, in particular, seem to have the best immunity and the longest life spans. While it is true that cats and kittens that have been rescued from colony situations, like Gucci, Valentino and Versace, could have picked up diseases such as feline immunodeficiency virus or feline leukaemia virus, in general the kittens that survive in those sorts of environments tend to be the hardiest. They have to be. So from my own personal experience, a cat is a cat with its own individual personality. If you love a cat just as it is, you will bring out its unique characteristics, as loving parents do with their different children. All sentient beings recognise love. Love makes everything blossom: humans, animals and plants. And if you adopt a rescue cat or kitten, you are saving a life.

Then, as my conversations with Halina often do, the talk turns to matters of the spirit. 'So many people these days lack purpose,' she tells me. 'They run from this activity to that, trying to find some meaning, but it always eludes them. I think this problem is unique to humans, not because we are more intelligent, but because we aren't really taught the true value of service anymore. In many ways we have to overcome our own selfishness. Bees have a purpose, worms have a purpose, even microbes have a purpose. If human beings vanished from the face of the earth, nature would carry on. But if the microbes disappeared we'd all be finished. A person needs a purpose, otherwise they are just a sort of useless energy sucker.' Then she tells me what she had read in the newspaper that morning about all the people emulating Kim Kardashian's Brazilian butt-lift surgery. 'Do you know, it has the highest fatality rate of any type of plastic surgery, but people still want it? Why? Why can't young women see how beautiful they already are and spend their energy doing more useful things with their lives? "Your bum is fine," I want to tell them, "so come and help me save animals".'

We have a giggle about that. Perhaps that would be a good slogan for the next WLPA volunteer drive: 'Your bum is fine! Come and help us save animals!' It's clear to me that Halina lives every day of her life with enormous purpose. If I told someone that my seventy-year-old friend lived on a property by herself with fifty cats, I can only imagine what they'd think. Her calling is not always easy; often it is exhausting and heartbreaking. But she never looks tired the way so many other people do, worn out by their mundane existence. Only a few days ago, I was watching people get on the 5.30pm train in Sydney's central business district. The commuters were far younger than Halina, but they looked completely drained of life. Halina's days are fuelled by passionate purpose. 'I spend my time helping the animals because I feel so much gratitude towards life,' she tells me. 'Growing up in post-war Germany was not always easy, but I'm thankful for all the opportunities that have come to me. I've seized every one of them. I want to live the rest of my life being useful.'

The day is marching on and Halina has so much to do. She has to feed all these cats then go and feed the colony cats she cares for too. Halina's first task is to call in all of the cats so she can lock them up in the cattery for the night, to keep them safe and warm and also to protect the wildlife. I love to watch how they run to her, the bold and the timid alike.

'Do you ever forget one?' I ask her. 'Have you accidentally ever locked one out?'

She gives me a smile. 'No, not really. I know when they are all inside and ready to be fed before settling down to sleep. I have a sixth sense for them.'

Dear Pebbles,

Why do people I meet at social occasions, once they find out I have cats, feel compelled to tell me how much they hate cats or put me down in some way? I don't tell people with kids that I don't like children.
Oppressed

Dear Oppressed,

Of course you don't tell people who have kids that you don't like children. Just as you don't tell the man who has a very obvious toupee that you don't like wigs, or inform Aunty May that you hate the crocheted jumpsuit she made for you last Christmas. You, Oppressed, are polite. Unfortunately, some people are not.

Politeness is a sign of intelligence, something cat haters lack. I suggest that you don't stoop to their level and don't try to convince them to change their opinion—they just want to lure you into an argument. So here are some suggested rejoinders that should be delivered with your sweetest, feline smile, so as to leave your oppressor wondering whether they've just been delivered a parting shot . . . or not.

For the dog enthusiast:

Them ⤔ *I prefer dogs. They are friendlier.*

You ⤔ *Indeed, I find cats very discerning about who they approach.*

For the cat critic:

Them ⤔ *Cats are lazy.*

You ⤔ *My cat does spend a lot of time contemplating things. I find him much more intelligent than a lot of people I meet.*

For the cat hater:

Them ⤔ *I hate cats!*

You ⤔ *Cats prefer intelligent, sensitive and warm people, so it's probably just as well.*

Then, turn your head, raise your tail and glissade away in a haughty manner to find someone more suited to your refined taste.

Pebbles

The felines appear, running from their hiding places towards Halina and the cattery door. They rub against her legs and greet her before hurrying inside. They seem to know that in her they have a heroine, an angel, a human mother. I get back into my car, feeling as though I've watched the queen of cats presiding over her little fairies. Indeed, it does feel like something ancient. I wonder if perhaps Halina might have been a witch in a past life, or a priestess for the goddess Bastet.

How to help our feline friends

There are hundreds of thousands of cats around the world living in terrible conditions. While feeding a stray cat is an act of kindness, one of the best ways to make a real difference is to support a cat charity or your local animal shelter. Not everyone is in a position to take in foster animals or care for sick kittens at home, but charities and shelters need all sorts of help, so the best thing to do is to contact one and let them know what your particular skills are and how much time you can devote. These are some of the skills that might come in handy:

♥ Secretarial and administrative

♥ Reception

♥ Social media and publicity

♥ Legal and legal correspondence

- ♥ Networking

- ♥ Fundraising

- ♥ Homemaking: would you be willing to do a few loads of washing a week? Clean some cages?

- ♥ Animal care: can you go to the shelter on a regular basis to play with kittens and young cats, to help familiarise them to social contact?

- ♥ Handyman or handywoman abilities

- ♥ Driving: can you help with deliveries? Could you transport animals from the shelter to the local veterinary surgery and back again?

But the most important attribute to have is commitment.

Joining an organisation is a great way to meet like-minded people and make friends. From my experience as a volunteer, here are some important things to keep in mind in order for you to contribute positively.

Leave your ego at the door and don't create more problems for the organisation than you solve ⊶
Be humble. Be good at what you are asked to do. Cooperate. You are there to help the animals, not work through your own self-importance issues.

Do your best to get along with the other volunteers ⊷ Everyone is there to do their best. Encourage your fellow volunteers and don't create interorganisational conflicts. Uplift everyone with your positive words and energy. The best way to help the animals is to care about the people who are trying to help them. If volunteers quit because you are too difficult to deal with, you haven't done any service to the animals.

Know your limits and stick to them ⊷ If you can only volunteer for a couple of hours a week or month, keep to that but do those hours supremely well. Be utterly reliable. It's better that you do that on a consistent basis than go flat chat, exhaust yourself and then quit.

Remember, you are the face of the organisation you represent ⊷ Be professional and polite at all times.

See the bigger picture ⊷ You may not be able to save the entire world, but if you can save one animal at a time, you are contributing in a truly meaningful way. Know that you are an important piece of a larger puzzle.

Other ways you can contribute to the wellbeing of cats and other animals include:

Take responsibility for your own cats ⇒⟶ Have them desexed and keep them contained, especially at night, in order to prevent cat fights, injuries and harm to local wildlife. Encourage your friends and family to do the same.

Don't own more cats than you can take good care of.

Become a regular donor to a cat charity ⇒⟶ You don't have to be a millionaire to do this. You can skip a couple of takeaway meals or coffees each month and still make a significant difference over time. Or you can organise your own events and get the guests to donate money towards a cat welfare organisation. You could ask your friends and family to donate to a charity on your behalf rather than give you birthday or Christmas gifts.

Include your cats and other companion animals in your will ⇒⟶ Make sure there are clear instructions about them and say who you trust to take responsibility for them. If you wish them to go to a shelter, provide funding for that shelter to be able to take care of them until they are rehomed. You can also leave a legacy from your estate to a cat charity or welfare organisation.

4
Cat magic

C ats, witches and magic have a long association. The connection originated in Egypt, with cat goddesses such as Bastet being associated with women's matters: fertility, the home, health and beauty. With the increase in trade, these deities were exported into European cultures where they morphed into pagan divinities, such as the Nordic goddess Freya who rode a chariot pulled by two black cats. But there were other reasons the relationship blossomed too. Witches were the village shamans and, like many spiritual practitioners, often preferred a solitary, contemplative existence. Who better to keep them company than the watchful, quiet cat? Witches were healers, too, and needed to store a variety of herbs and natural medicines. A cat companion would keep vermin away.

Yet cats, perhaps more than any other domesticated animal, seem to possess divine qualities all of their own. These characteristics make them the perfect partners in creating magic.

♥ Cats are mysterious and so is the Divine.

♥ They stalk silently and often appear next to us, unheard.

♥ They are regal and beautiful to behold.

♥ They can balance gracefully and leap to high places.

♥ They can't be forced to do anything. They need to be coaxed, cultivated and charmed—just like magic!

♥ They hear things we can't.

♥ They can see in the dark and travel by the light of the moon.

♥ Their whiskers are exquisitely sensitive and help them negotiate tight spaces and even detect changes in air currents to warn them of danger.

♥ They communicate in a language of scents.

♥ They are watchful and patient when the situation calls for it. At other times, they are curious and playful.

If we take magic to mean miraculous events that cannot be explained by natural or scientific laws, do you have to be a practising white witch in order to conjure magic with your cat? My answer to that is no. I have met many beautiful Wiccans and have even had the privilege of joining in with their sacred rituals, but I don't believe Wicca is the only path to a magical life.

In my experience, magic is not so much something that you do, it is something that you are. It is your entire way of being in the world. To live a magical life that incorporates your feline companion, you don't need herbs and tools so much as you need to hold the following beliefs:

A deep sense of the Divine ⇢ The conviction that there is an invisible force of goodness and love that is much bigger than the physical world you see. (You can call it anything you like; for example, The Divine, God, your Higher Power, The Universe.)

The belief that you are part of this Presence ⇢ That it exists not only outside of you but inside you too.

The belief that all other living beings are part of this Presence too ⇢ Your feline companion is here with you now on this part of your journey for a very specific reason: as a comforter, a guide or a teacher.

The belief that you create magic in collaboration with this Presence ⊷⟶ You cannot control it, cajole it or force it to do your bidding. You work in cooperation with it by taking responsibility for the natural and trusting it to perform the supernatural in magnificent ways that you can't even imagine.

In order to perform feline magic, you need to cultivate the following qualities daily:

Love ⊷⟶ A deep reverence for the Divine force, for yourself, for life and for all of the other living forms around you, especially your magical feline companion, your furry familiar.

Gratitude ⊷⟶ Appreciation is the spark that gives your magic its power. Why? Because gratitude instantly connects you to the Divine.

Trust ⊷⟶ Trust the Divine's love for you. A great mantra for this mindset is 'Life is always happening for me, never against me.' Know that while you may have your heart set on a particular goal, the Divine may have an even better, more wonderful plan for you. Or it may be taking you to where you want to be, but on a path you don't expect. Always be prepared for this and always continue to trust. This is a journey you are making and resistance to that will always cause you more pain and suffering than if you surrendered to guidance.

Willingness to be open ⟶ Open your heart and mind to guidance from the Divine and develop your own intuition as well.

How to make magic with your cat

Kitty altar

An altar will give your magic an important focal point in your home. It should consist of items that put you in a magical state of mind, filled with happiness and a sense of possibility. Things that could go on your altar include:

♥ A photograph of your beloved cat(s).

♥ A statue of a feline goddess—Bastet, Artemis, Diana or Freya, for example—or a favourite cat ornament if you prefer.

♥ Things with your favourite colours or scents: flowers, candles, crystals, herbs.

♥ A beautiful journal with a cat picture on it in which you can write down inspirational quotes, ideas, affirmations, gratitude lists, dreams, goals and intentions.

♥ The ashes of a beloved cat, which are very magical, in a beautiful urn or box. Only include this if you are at peace with the passing of your cat; if it makes you feel sad, it belongs in another sacred place in your house, but not on your altar.

This altar can be set up on a table, windowsill or shelf. If you are unable to have a permanent altar, you can keep these items in a special box and bring them out when you want to meditate on and visualise your goals and desires.

Your altar is a focal point to infuse yourself with the energy of your intention to live your life beautifully and magically. For this reason you should spend some time before it every day, focusing peacefully and joyfully on your goals and intentions. Even five minutes spent at the altar in the morning will magically energise you in preparation for the day. With your current cat companion in your arms or nearby, study the items on the altar one by one and visualise your goal, dream or intention for the day. See it as already complete. When you finish, stroke your cat three times to ground the magic.

As you go about your day, watch for synchronicities, signs and unexpected good luck; dreams you'd almost given up on suddenly coming to fruition; unexpected healings; and people giving you the guidance and help you need. When these come up, be sure to express your gratitude to the Divine: this will increase your magic tenfold!

Nikola Tesla

SERBIAN-AMERICAN INVENTOR (1856–1943)

Nikola Tesla's childhood companion was a black cat
named Macak. Tesla was to credit Macak as the
inspiration for his lifelong interest in electricity.
One evening when he was stroking the cat's back,
he saw Macak's fur light up. Tesla's hand produced
sparks loud enough to be heard all over the house.
His mother joked that he should stop playing
with the cat lest he set the house alight, but Tesla
was already pondering the origins of energy.
Was nature just a gigantic cat being stroked
by God to produce electricity?

Cat charms

A charm is an object that you imbue with magic by using it to focus your desires and intentions. Charms that can incorporate your cat's magic into the mix include:

A love-heart locket with a snip of your cat's fur in it ➤——➤ This is a great charm to wear when you need confidence and optimism. It will remind you that you love and are deeply loved. Everything will work out for you in the long run. There is a special being waiting at home for you who sees you with eyes of pure love.

A vial with your cat's trimmed claw in it ➤——➤ When you are next trimming your cat's claws, keep one of the sharpened points in a vial that you can carry in your pocket, handbag or even wear around your neck if you like. It will serve to remind you that sometimes you have to be assertive (to fight for your territory) and to go after what you want and catch it. There is a time for being patient and a time for being active. This cat charm will turn you into a hunter and a fighter. This is also a great charm for protection.

One of your cat's shed whiskers ➤——➤ Traditionally these were considered good-luck talismans because cats don't shed their whiskers often. You can keep one inside your purse or tape it to your computer monitor, diary or calendar to bring you luck with a work project or event. You can also use a whisker as a charm when you have to do any sort of negotiation. Cats' whiskers are navigation aids and emotional barometers. This charm will help you heighten your own senses and your inner intuition, and encourage you to ask pertinent questions. It will remind you to study people and listen to your intuition before you trust them. (Please note, these must always be shed whiskers. Never cut or pluck your cat's whiskers: they are highly sensitive! You will invite harm on yourself if you hurt your kitty.)

Asking for guidance

All practitioners of magic understand that everything that comes into our life comes for a reason. All of the cats you have had in your life were there to help you along on your journey. You can absolutely ask for guidance from a beloved cat that has passed. If this is a recently departed companion, allow the worst of your grief to heal first. This will create a clearer connection in asking for guidance. Beloved cats are good at giving guidance for things that will bring you happiness; for example, a fresh direction in your life, such as a new job or new friendships. They are great guides for when you feel low and don't know how to help yourself. If you need guidance on very practical matters, it is better to ask for the help of a passed beloved human such as a parent or grandparent. Cats are not very practical in this life or the next. But they certainly know how to love and how to enjoy themselves!

♥ Pick a quiet spot, especially if it is a place that has a deep association with your beloved cat.

♥ Breathe in and out slowly and deeply until your mind stills and a sense of calm and peace washes over you.

♥ See in your mind's eye your cat and imagine both of you surrounded by a circle of bright white light.

♥ Bathe in the feeling of love between you.

♥ Recall some good times you shared with your cat when they were in physical form and thank it for those times.

♥ Ask it for the guidance you seek.

♥ When you feel ready, send your beloved cat love, say 'thank you' and open your eyes.

As you go through your day, stay alert for signs, synchronicities and encouraging events that come to you and remember to say 'thank you'.

Tarot card readings

If you enjoy tarot card reading, you can incorporate your cat into readings by letting them choose the cards. When you spread out the deck, let kitty choose with a sniff or a touch of a paw. Just remember, you will have to be patient and not force your cat.

Even if your cat just sits with you while you do your readings, it will help with clarity and increase your wisdom in interpreting the meanings and how to apply them in your life.

Burying troubles

What does a cat do with its poop? It buries it! You can do the same with the memory of any embarrassing, disappointing or unpleasant event that has happened to you during the day, in order to stop dwelling on it and move on to creating some positive magic in your life instead.

Take a piece of paper and write down what happened and how it made you feel. Spend a moment reliving all the awkward and uncomfortable feelings that you associate with that event. Then cut up the paper into tiny segments and mix them in with your cat's litter. Let your kitty do the rest when it is ready. Then scoop up the soiled paper along with the litter and get rid of it. As you do, say three times, 'I let this sh_t go so I can get on with creating the positive experiences I want. It is done. I let it go.'

Never partake in this spell maliciously or with anger. It works best when performed with a sense of humour. Never do it with somebody's photograph. You are altering your own perception of an event, not trying to harm or take revenge on somebody else!

Magic in tough times

It is easy to appreciate magic when life is going well and everything is flowing beautifully. But when challenges arise, it does not mean that the magic has disappeared. Living consciously means that you will avoid a lot of unnecessary conflict and distress through your awareness and by responding to life events and people instead of reacting to them. But no life will be without dark times. It is part of our existence here in our physical bodies, just as we have the contrasts between day and night and the seasons. In the same way gravity gives us the resistance we need to keep our muscles and bones strong, so challenges serve to strengthen us if we allow them to do so.

To access magic in sad and challenging times, your cat is the perfect companion. A cat's purr is usually associated with contentment. But cats also purr when they are frightened, sick,

When I play with my cat, who knows whether she isn't amusing herself with me more than I am with her?
Montaigne (French philosopher, 1533–1592)

injured or giving birth. It is a self-comforting mechanism, but it is also being researched as a possible healing mechanism. Cats purr at a frequency between 25 and 150 Hertz. The sound frequencies in this range could possibly be used to improve bone density and promote muscle healing. Various studies have shown that people who interact with their cats have lowered stress hormones and healthier blood pressure and they are less likely to die of a heart attack.

Your cat is a healing presence. So in dark times, make a special nook for you and your cat to commune together on a daily basis. If your cat is affectionate, take full advantage of this. Let your cat rub you and curl up to you and paw you. If your cat isn't so affectionate, simply sit with them and enjoy their graceful presence and connection.

If your cat starts purring at this time, close your eyes and bring yourself into the full mindfulness of that purr. Breathe naturally but keep your mind focused on the purr and feel it penetrate into your own body, mind and heart.

This time—even fifteen minutes to half an hour each day—will be sacred to you as part of your healing journey. Be gentle with yourself, especially if you are experiencing grief or have received a worrying diagnosis, or when distressing global events cause you to feel fearful of the future. When you begin to feel calmer and stronger, you can take out your journal and use this time to ask your intuition certain questions and to write the answers in your journal.

- ♥ What is the best thing I can do to comfort and support myself through this challenge?

- ♥ What insights are there for me to gain from this situation?

- ♥ What is the next step I should take?

- ♥ Is there anything I should be doing now to prepare myself for when I move past this challenge?

Don't force any answers to these questions. They may come up immediately or sometimes hours, days or even months later. Let the answers spring up naturally but put the request out there.

Challenges frighten us and take away our peace. Our task in magic is to find the calm eye in the middle of the storm as much as we can, even if we can only manage that peace for the short time we spend in comforting meditation with our cat.

By communing calmly with your cat and asking for Divine guidance, you will find that you are led step by step through a process that is healing and strengthening, even though at times it also feels overwhelming and daunting. There will come a time when you realise that you have been led through the dark, deep woods and out into the sunshine again: you will find that the magic never went away, as it was with you all along. And your furry spirit friend was only too happy to help you on that journey.

5

Natural therapies for cats

A s more people turn to holistic medicine for healing, there is a growing interest in how natural therapies may benefit cats. Some therapies and home remedies are considered safe for cats, but there are always three rules to follow in seeking care for your beloved animal companion.

Conventional veterinary medical advice should always be sought first ➤— This is especially important if your cat is showing symptoms of illness, including vomiting, diarrhoea, bleeding or any sign of disorientation or pain. A good veterinarian will be able to diagnose your cat's illness far more accurately than you can. Even if the illness is serious, early medical attention often means that the treatment will be less invasive and complicated and will have a better outcome than late-stage diagnosis. If you decide to use alternative medicine as well, then you will know exactly what disease you are treating.

Always inform your veterinarian about the natural therapies you intend to use or are using on your cat ►——→ Even some seemingly innocuous therapies such as nutritional supplements could interfere with the efficacy of any medical treatments your cat is currently receiving; for example, antioxidant supplements should not be given if your cat is undergoing chemotherapy, as they may reduce the effectiveness of the medications. If your current veterinarian doesn't support your desire to include complementary medicine in the care of your cat, you can find one who does so that they can advise you properly. That way you can work as a team to give your cat the best possible attention.

Don't assume that what is good for you, will be good for your cat ►——→ Some therapies, such as certain essential oils and herbs (for example, St John's wort and comfrey), can be toxic to cats.

Your cat's health

Stress

The principle requirements of good health that apply to humans apply to cats as well. These include exercise, adequate sleep (Hah! I hear you say), quality food and fresh water. Stress can have the same detrimental, disease-causing effect on cats as it does on their guardians. As your cat doesn't have to go to work, pay bills or deal with in-laws, you may well wonder what on earth your cat could be stressed about! But common stressors for cats include:

♥ Living with a bully cat or dog (or child for that matter).

♥ Not enough territory of its own in your home.

♥ The arrival of a new person or animal or the departure of a beloved human or animal companion.

♥ Home renovations.

♥ Strong-smelling chemicals in the home, including perfumes, cigarette smoke and heavily scented candles.

♥ Moving to a new home.

♥ A constantly dirty litterbox.

♥ Arguing and tension among the humans in the house.

Common symptoms of stress in cats

As these symptoms can also indicate a serious underlying illness, it's best to get your cat checked by a veterinarian if it is displaying any of these signs.

♥ Eliminating outside the litterbox

♥ Aggression towards other human or animal family members

♥ Stomach upsets

♥ Overgrooming, to the point of creating bald spots in the fur

♥ Not grooming at all so that the fur becomes matted and greasy-looking

♥ Infections: bladder, eye, skin, etc

♥ Always hiding

If no underlying cause can be found, you can take the following steps to reduce the stressors in your cat's environment. The first step to reducing your cat's anxiety is to deal with any stressors in its environment. Create safe hideaways for your cat to retreat to away from noise and other animals. Boxes with blankets in them make attractive hideaways when they are tucked under chairs, placed in quiet corners or on top of cupboards (cats often feel more secure when they can observe the world from above). You don't have to move to a larger home to provide adequate territory in multi-cat households where the cats are showing signs of stress. (Just don't add any more animals to the mix.) You can create more territory for your cats by providing greater vertical space in the form of cat towers, wall-mounted perches, beds on top of cupboards and designated chairs. Vertical territory is more important to cats than horizontal territory.

Make sure your cat has stress-free access to its litterbox and food, too. The rule for litterboxes in multi-cat households is one per cat plus one. If your stressed cat is being bullied by another one, put the stressed cat's litterbox where it can access it without being ambushed. You should also feed your stressed cat away from other animals who might steal its food.

Kick the habit, not the cat

Second-hand smoke from cigarettes, cigars and marijuana is as dangerous for cats as it is for humans, not only because of the effects on their small lungs, but also because the smoke residue they lick off their fur (known as third-hand smoke) is toxic to them. The danger to their health increases with prolonged exposure. Another good reason to give up smoking!

Cats are very clean animals. A filthy litterbox is as off-putting to a cat as a disgusting public toilet is to you! If you have a single cat but spend long hours away from home, give the cat two litterboxes so a clean one is always available for it to use.

If your cat is grieving the loss of an animal companion, don't immediately introduce it to another animal. Rather, give it more attention and kindness. Feed it food it especially likes, groom it, allow it to sleep with you if it wants. This is the same if it has lost a beloved human companion.

Synthetic cat pheromones can help relieve stress. You can spray these a couple of times a day in the spaces where your cat spends most of its time.

Provide quality food to make sure your cat is getting good nutrition and plenty of fresh water daily (cats drink more when stressed). Play with your cat using toys it enjoys (not toys that make it feel more stressed or frightened). Just as with humans, fun is great for stress relief.

One of the best ways to care for your cat's wellbeing is to take good care of your own. Cats are highly sensitive and will pick up tension and fear from you. Have you ever noticed that neurotic animals often have neurotic owners? By practising good self-care and self-love, you will keep a clear, happy and healthy connection between you and your cat.

Natural therapies for stress

* Bach Flower Remedies. Rescue Remedy works for cats too, but make sure you use the one especially formulated for pets.
* Music therapy. Played at a low volume, soothing music at slow tempos can help calm your cat. Research has shown that cats recover faster from surgery when classical music is played in the background. You can purchase music especially compiled for cats or try Samuel Barber's 'Adagio for Strings' or Bach's 'Air on the G String'.
* A pot of catnip. At first this will give your cat a pleasurable high. But eventually your cat will calm down and simply feel good. Catnip is harmless to your cat and is non-addictive; just don't let your cat drive or operate machinery while under the influence!
* Homeopathy. Must be prescribed by a qualified naturopathic veterinarian; the wrong treatment could harm your cat.

Digestive issues

Digestive issues, including vomiting, diarrhoea, constipation and any sign of pain or strain when eliminating, should be checked by a veterinarian first to rule out serious illness. Once your cat has been given the all clear, nutritional supplements may be helpful in maintaining your cat's intestinal health.

Plain psyllium powder (fine) works well for both constipation and diarrhoea ➤——➤ Mix a quarter of a teaspoon into your cat's wet food twice a day. Psyllium powder needs adequate liquid or there is a risk of your cat choking, so don't sprinkle it on dry food or use more than the above amount. If your cat has been prescribed any medicine, don't give it at the same time as psyllium powder, as it may not be absorbed properly.

Slippery elm powder can be good for the nausea that often accompanies inflammatory bowel disease or kidney disease ➤——➤ Using a whisk or fork, stir one teaspoon of good-quality slippery elm powder into half a cup of water in a saucepan. Bring to a simmer and keep stirring until the mixture thickens to a syrup. The mixture will thicken further as it cools and can be stored in the refrigerator for up to three days. Add half a teaspoon to your cat's wet food two to three times a day. If your cat doesn't like the taste, try a smaller amount at first and gradually build up. Don't administer a medication at the same time as giving the syrup, as the medication may not be properly absorbed. (Tip: good-quality slippery elm should taste sweet, not bitter, so you might want to do a taste test first before giving the syrup to your kitty.)

Probiotics can be helpful for cats with digestive issues such as constipation and diarrhoea ⟶ Make sure you purchase a good-quality formulation that is suitable for cats.

Age-related issues
As with humans, elderly cats can experience a general decline in health that is not life-threatening, but can impact the quality of their life.

Omega-3 fatty acids can be beneficial in treating arthritis and easing kidney disease ⟶ Sometimes diets specially formulated for these conditions will already contain omega-3 fatty acids. If you want to add supplements to your cat's diet, consult your veterinarian for the correct dosage for your cat and its condition.

An injection of vitamin B12 from your veterinarian may give your elderly cat a new lease of life ⟶ Cats cannot produce their own B12 and an elderly cat may not be absorbing enough of the vitamin through its digestive tract. This is especially true for cats with chronic bowel disorders such as inflammatory bowel disease. A shot of B12 may stimulate the appetite of a cat suffering from kidney disease.

Walking therapy ➤——➤ An elderly cat may wish to sleep all day. As long as your feline companion isn't in pain, walking an elderly cat around your garden on a lead is a great way to reduce stiffness in its joints and keep its mind and senses stimulated as it sniffs flowers and those mysterious scents carried on the breeze that only cats can detect. It's also a nice way to spend time with a beloved companion in its later years.

Heat therapy ➤——➤ Frail, elderly cats may not be able to produce enough body heat. A warm, but not hot, heat pad may give them some pain relief and comfort in winter.

Fleas

Fleas are harmful to cats not only because they make them itch, but also because they carry life-threatening diseases such as heartworm.

Indoor cats rarely contract fleas, so you can usually spare them chemical spot-on treatments unless they are going to stay at cat accommodation while you go on holiday. But fleas can still make their way into a home on people's clothing, on untreated dogs or under doors and through windows, so you should check your cat regularly for any evidence of flea dirt. The best way to stop a flea infestation in your home is to vacuum regularly, especially in dark places such as in corners, under sofa cushions and behind furniture.

If your cat is allergic to chemical spot-on preparations for fleas, there are some natural treatments you can try.

Daily combing with a flea comb ➤—→ Fleas multiply at a rapid rate, so you may have to comb three times a day to keep on top of them. Cover all the places fleas like to hide: around the neck, under the legs and the base of the tail. Drown the fleas in a bowl of soapy water. When you are done, soak a washcloth in a diluted solution of apple cider vinegar, wring it out and wipe over your cat. In winter, let your cat dry off in a warm room.

Keep your cat clean ➤—→ Regularly wash your cat's bedding and hang it in the sun to dry. If your cat will tolerate a bath, use a gentle cat shampoo. Leave the shampoo on for as long as your cat will allow, as the detergent in the shampoo will kill fleas—five minutes is ideal. Use a diluted solution of apple cider vinegar as the final rinse. Wash from the head towards the tail, so the fleas can't take refuge on your cat's head.

Brewer's yeast ➤—→ You can add half a teaspoon of brewer's yeast to your cat's wet food daily. Some enthusiasts swear that this makes their cat taste bad to fleas, plus it also provides some nutritional value to the cat. Some cats are allergic to brewer's yeast, so proceed with caution and stop using it if your cat has a reaction.

If you have found fleas on your cat, it may have contracted worms, so the safest precaution is to treat it. Consult with your veterinarian about the best approach to worming your cat, especially if it is very young, has a health condition or is elderly. Worms can undermine your cat's health and lead to serious illness and there are no known home remedies that are one hundred per cent effective against them.

Unfortunately there are no known, safe natural prevention treatments for the deadly Australian paralysis tick. The best protection is to keep your cat indoors. If your cat spends time free-roaming, in an outdoor enclosure or being walked by you on a lead outside in tick-prone areas, you will need to use veterinarian-recommended tick protection. If you like to garden or bushwalk during the warmer months, it's wise to use insect repellent on yourself and clean your shoes and clothing before you enter your home to avoid inadvertently bringing ticks inside. Should you find a paralysis tick on your cat, removing it is not enough. You must seek veterinary assistance urgently, as the tick will have injected toxins into your cat's bloodstream. The more quickly you act, the better the outcome is likely to be.

Other therapies

You may have found acupressure, reiki and other non-invasive therapies beneficial for yourself and would like to try these complementary healing modalities on your cat; however, if travelling to a practitioner is highly stressful for your cat, you may be negating any good the therapy will do. You can always ask if home visits are an option. In addition there are skills you can learn, such as therapeutic massage for your cat.

Blessings and prayers

The Divine is as interested in the welfare of your cat as you are. You can use this connection to bring healing and wellbeing to your cat.

During the Feast of St Francis of Assisi, a celebration of the Roman Catholic church's patron saint of animals, church officials sometimes bless animals of all descriptions.

Leaders of pagan covens, Buddhist priests, other spiritual healers and even your friends can all be asked to pray or perform spells, chants or rituals for your cat. And don't forget that you have a direct connection to the Divine too! Angelic help is available in the form of the archangel Raphael, who is said to be a powerful healer of both animals and their human guardians.

Leonor Fini

ARGENTINE ARTIST, DESIGNER
AND AUTHOR (1907–1996)

Leonor Fini and her numerous Persian cats moved
as a pack. Where she ate, they ate. Where she slept,
they slept. When she went on summer holidays to the
Loire Valley, they came with her in their own separate
car. But Fini was never a loner who only desired the
company of her cats. She is reported to have said that
marriage never appealed to her; she wanted to live
in a big house with her cats and friends. Fini and
Brigitte Bardot were good friends and animal activists
in France, and Fini used her fame to help draw
attention to the plight of stray cats.

Massage for cats

If your cat likes being touched, then massaging your cat can be beneficial for both you and your cat. Massage helps stimulate your cat's circulation and lymphatic system. Touching your cat in a way that gives it pleasure will make it more trusting of you for those occasions when your touch doesn't mean pleasure; for example, when you have to administer a pill, trim your cat's nails or apply a spot-on treatment. As an extra bonus, massaging your cat can reduce stress hormones in your own body and help protect against heart disease by lowering your blood pressure and reducing your heart rate. (Tip: don't massage your cat if it has very recently undergone surgery. Wait until your veterinarian gives you the go-ahead before doing so.)

- Pick a time when your cat is relaxed: dozing is fine, but not fast asleep. Nobody enjoys being woken up!

- Make the environment around you as peaceful as possible.

- You can brush your cat before massaging it. This will stop you breathing in a lot of fur as you work.

- Take a few deep breaths and get yourself into a positive state of mind by thinking of all the reasons why you are grateful for your cat. This will allow you to channel healing, loving energy towards your cat.

♥ Get your cat ready for your touch by rubbing the parts of its body where you know it likes to be touched: under the chin, around the neck, etc.

♥ Start with very short sessions and gradually build up to longer ones as your cat gets used to being massaged. Even if your cat only accepts a back massage for a few days, that is still a great start.

♥ Don't be offended if your cat gets up and walks off. Try again later.

How to give your cat a massage
Pat your cat with light, slow strokes that move in the direction of its fur as a preparation for the massage. This will allow your cat to become accustomed to your touch. You can also speak softly to your cat at this point and tell it how much you love it and that you want to give it a lovely massage.

Start the massage on your cat's back, moving from the nape of the neck down the column of the spine to the base of the tail. Don't massage the spine itself—that could hurt your cat—rather run your thumb and index finger down the muscles on either

The more you rub a cat on the rump, the higher she sets her tail.

Proverb (mid-seventeenth century)

side of the spine. If your cat likes this, repeat this move several times gradually increasing your pressure. Note that some cats like being touched at the base of the tail and others hate it. If your cat doesn't like it, decrease the pressure in this spot.

Now move your massage to the cat's head, neck and chest. Hold your index and middle fingers together and gently press small sections at a time with tiny circular motions. You should feel the cat's skin move easily over the muscles underneath. If your cat doesn't like too much pressure around its face and head, use long strokes in those areas instead of circular motions. Don't put pressure at all on the throat, but use gentle stroking motions.

Massage your cat's shoulders and forelegs. Use only gentle pressure around joints and stop if your cat shows any sign of pain. When massaging the limbs, you can use your thumb on one side of the limb and your index and middle fingers on the other; this will allow you to hold the limb steady. Some cats do not like their paws or paw pads touched, as they are very sensitive. If this is the case, leave your cat's paws alone or lightly touch them and slowly build up to touching them for longer with each successive massage.

Continue with circular motions along your cat's sides and use long strokes along its abdomen. Be careful not to press too hard on its internal organs. Make note of any signs of pain or lumps.

Massage your cat's hips and hind legs the same way you massaged its shoulders and forelimbs.

Cat wisdom

Coco

'Don't let anyone steal your sparkle . . . or your cat toy!'

Most cats don't like having their tails touched, so leave that part alone.

Finish the massage with long strokes from the head down the back, from the shoulders down the front limbs to the paws, down the chest, from the hips down the legs to the paws, and from the front of the face towards the back. You can use your flat palm for the larger areas and your closed fingers for smaller areas. Use slow, firm strokes.

Thank your cat for the time you have spent together. Wish it health, happiness and wellbeing. If your cat wants to sleep, let it. And if you need a nap too, go right ahead!

At the florist

Never send lilies to a friend with a cat. If someone gives you lilies, thank them, but pass them on to someone without a cat. These flowers look and smell beautiful, but they are deadly to cats. Every part of this flower, from the pollen to the petals, is dangerous and can cause acute kidney failure if even very small amounts are ingested. The cat doesn't have to eat the flower or its parts to suffer. If it were to brush against the pollen or get some on its fur or paw and then lick itself, it could become dangerously ill within hours. When sending flowers, always let your florist know that the receiver has a cat (or other companion animal) and to not send anything toxic to them. (Peace lilies as house plants are safe, as they are not true lilies.)

Toxic		Safe	
✘	Hyacinths	✓	Roses
✘	Hydrangeas	✓	Sunflowers
✘	Poinsettia (watch out at Christmas!)	✓	Carnations
		✓	Snapdragons
✘	Tulips (the bulbs)	✓	Gerberas
✘	Cyclamen	✓	Zinnias
✘	Daffodils	✓	Asters
✘	Chrysanthemums	✓	Orchids

6

Communicating with your cat

C ats are whole-body communicators. To understand what your cat is telling you, look at its eyes, ears, whiskers, tail and body. Listen to its vocalisations as well.

Body language

Eyes

Not only are your cat's eyes beautiful, but they are also highly efficient. Your cat's visual field is greater than yours and that possessed glowing look that emanates from its eyes in the dark is due to a reflective layer behind the retina that maximises the amount of light available and offers superior vision in dim light conditions.

'The eyes are the windows to the soul' is a perfect metaphor for describing your cat's optical organs. Understanding your cat's gaze is a great way to tell what it is thinking.

Slightly oval pupils ➤⎯⎯➤ This is a sign of relaxation.

Droopy lids accompanied by blinks ➤⎯⎯➤ Trust and affection. This is how your cat conveys that it loves you. You can tell your cat you love it back by sending it the same slow blink.

A direct unblinking stare at you or another cat ➤⎯⎯➤ Watch out! This signals danger. The cat is either displaying dominance or it feels threatened.

Round pupils that seem to make the iris disappear ➤⎯⎯➤ This is intense excitement: either the cat is about to launch into a playful frolic or it is displaying defensive aggression. Look at the rest of the body to work out which: an inverted 'u' shape to the tail suggests play; a fluffy tail and drawn-back ears mean trouble is brewing!

A cat has colour vision, limited to blues and greys and perhaps yellow and green. While your cat's peripheral vision is better than yours (it will spot a spider crawling up the wall faster), they don't have the muscles necessary to change the shape of their eye lenses, so they can't see things as clearly up close.

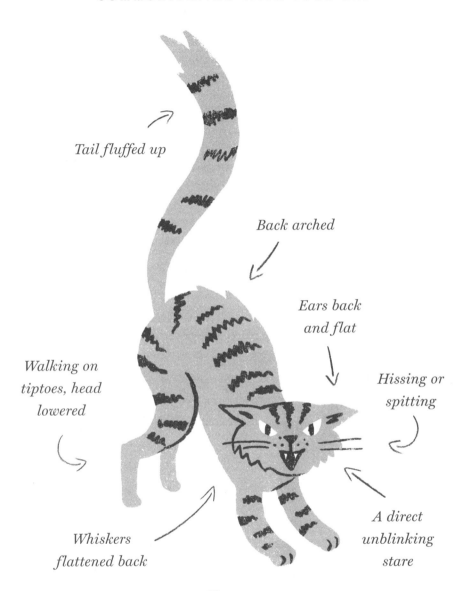

Tail fluffed up

Back arched

Ears back and flat

Walking on tiptoes, head lowered

Hissing or spitting

Whiskers flattened back

A direct unblinking stare

Angry

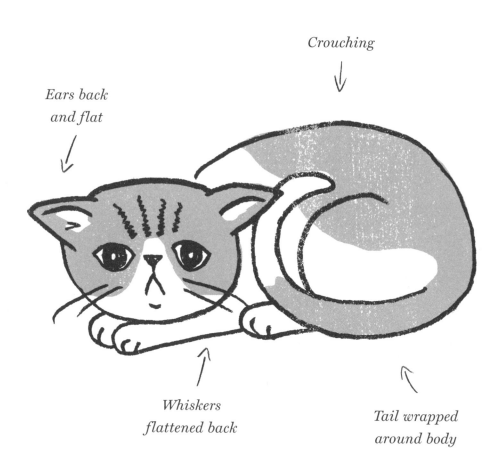

Crouching

Ears back
and flat

Whiskers
flattened back

Tail wrapped
around body

Fearful

Ears

You might be fascinated at how your cat can rotate its ears independently of each other in order to pinpoint the exact source of a sound. What a skill to have! Your cat can use one ear to stay aware of what is going on in one part of the room while tracking the sound in another; a distinct advantage at any cocktail party, to be sure. Ears are also the way your cat indicates its mood.

Perky and facing forward ➻⟶ Alert and interested.

Back and flat ➻⟶ Do not approach a cat with his ears in this position. It is feeling threatened and will attack if approached. Flattening its ears is how your cat protects these precious organs in a fight.

Tail

Your cat's tail is an extension of its spine, so be gentle with it. Don't grab it or tug on it. It has an important role in your cat's ability to balance. It is also a powerful mood indicator.

Horizontal ➻⟶ Neutral position.

Erect and curled at the tip like a question mark ➻⟶ This is an extremely friendly gesture. Your cat wants to approach you and usually follows up with headbutting and rubbing against your legs.

Wrapped around the body ➤—→ A touch wary and not in the mood to interact.

Between the legs ➤—→ The cat is timid and submissive.

Flicking ➤—→ Irritated or frustrated.

Lashing ➤—→ A sign of agitation.

Thumping ➤—→ The cat is in a bad mood.

Fluffed up like a skunk's tail ➤—→ This is a very anxious cat that is either ready for defence or attack.

Whiskers

While the discovery of whiskers sprouting from her face will send almost any cat lady running to the nearest beauty salon for therapy, whiskers are vital devices for your cat. The whisker follicles are highly sensitive. Because a cat doesn't see objects up close well, it uses its whiskers to detect movement—an extremely important advantage when it has captured prey (or preferably a toy). The whiskers help a cat navigate when the light is dim by detecting air currents, and they allow a cat to assess if it is really going to be able squeeze itself into that tight space behind the sofa when a stranger comes into the house. You can also tell your cat's state of mind from what their whiskers are doing.

Meowing,
trilling or
murmuring

Ears perky
and facing
forward

Tail curled
at the tip like
a question
mark

Whiskers
straight out
to the side

Droopy
lids and
slow
blinking

Happy

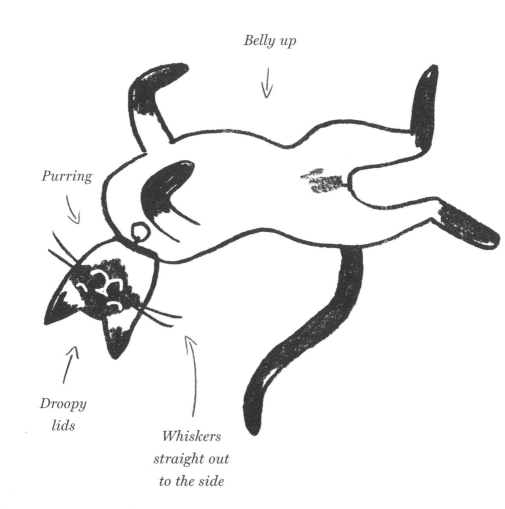

Belly up

Purring

Droopy
lids

Whiskers
straight out
to the side

Relaxed

Straight out to the side ➤⟶ The neutral, relaxed position.

Fanned forward ➤⟶ The cat is intensely interested and possibly about to pounce.

Flattened back ➤⟶ The cat is fearful.

And what about those whiskery eyebrows on your cat? These trigger blinking to protect its eyes when your cat moves through bushes.

Fur

While we need hairspray or gel to make our hair stand on end, your cat's fight-or-flight system will send hormonal signals to the muscles in its skin that say: 'Puff up! Danger coming!' A fluffed up cat is a frightened cat. It is trying to make itself appear bigger than it is to scare off a potential predator. The fancy term for this is 'piloerection'.

Body

Just as we can tell whether someone is confident or timid from their posture, the position of your cat's body communicates its state of mind.

Walking on tiptoes, head lowered ➤⟶ An aggressive or hunting stance.

Crouching ➤—→ The cat is fearful and on the defensive. It is trying to avoid being noticed by making itself as small as it can.

Arched back ➤—→ The cat is ready to react offensively or defensively.

Belly up ➤—→ This is a friendly position when the cat is in a relaxed state, especially if your cat is welcoming you home or is lying in the sunshine, but a cat will also roll on its back in a fight so it can utilise the claws on all four of its paws. This is where people get confused between cats and dogs. When a dog rolls over it wants its tummy scratched. A cat in a similar relaxed state might tolerate a tummy rub for a little while, but if you continue too long you will stimulate it into an attack state and it will claw or bite your hand. When your cat displays its tummy, appreciate that it is showing you that it trusts you, but pat it on the head or scratch it under the chin rather than touching its stomach. Or you could simply speak affectionately to it.

Rolling side to side ➤—→ Your cat is in love with you! This is a good time to grab your cat's toys and have a play together.

Vocalisations

Your cat will have its own repertoire of sounds that it makes with you. Try to understand the sound in relation to the context. At what times does your cat make this sound? What does its body language tell you about its mood? Then, if the vocalisation is a positive one, you might try to imitate the sound back to your cat. My cats Valentino, Versace and Gucci all have a variation of a 'mrrh' greeting they give me when I come home. I find that if I send that sound back to them, they get a look on their faces as if to say that I have paid them the highest compliment by attempting to communicate in cat lingo! Perhaps they feel gratified, the same way the native speakers of a country do when visitors attempt to learn the local language. Although it is tempting sometimes, I never make aggressive cat sounds at my cats, like hisses or snarls. Trust is a precious thing between a human and their cat and you should avoid frightening your cat, unless it is about to do something dangerous, such as jump onto a hot stove!

The one positive sound I have never managed to imitate competently is a cat's purr. That noise comes from muscles around the cat's larynx: as the cat breathes in and out, the muscles dilate and constrict the glottis, causing the air to vibrate. For me, it's about as complicated as playing the didgeridoo!

Dear Pebbles,

Recently I met a very handsome gentleman who seemed right for me in so many ways. Things were ticking along nicely until he suddenly became very jealous of the attention I lavish on my cat, Romeo. Sure Romeo has his own social media accounts and had a star named after him for his tenth birthday, but Romeo has been with me through thick and thin. Now my boyfriend has given me the ultimatum: 'It's me or the cat!' What should I do?
Torn Between Two Lovers

Dear Torn Between Two Lovers,
Rest assured that almost every true cat lady will be given this ultimatum at least once in her lifetime. If you internet search the subject 'It's me or the cat', you will see that almost every true cat lady chooses her cat in the end! Why is this? Because they know, deep in their hearts, that if someone really cares about them, they aren't likely to ask them to give up something they love so much. If you give up Romeo, he will just be the beginning of a long list of things you will be asked to sacrifice for the sake of the relationship. Secure men don't get jealous of your cat! Nor do they get jealous of

your relationship with your sister, your best friend, your mother or even your hairdresser!

So, Torn Between Two Lovers, I think you already know the answer to your own question. As hard as it is to believe, it's important to accept that there are people who really do not like cats and that life for you would be a trifle joyless with such a person. In the future, try to get this sorted out on the first date before emotions become involved. Show your potential beau pictures of Romeo, waft some of his fur around to see if your date sneezes, and ask questions; for example, 'Have you ever had a cat companion? Did you let your cat sleep in your bed? Do you have any animal companions now? What are their names? What is your favourite designer animal clothing store?' If your date runs a mile, have faith that there is someone better suited to you . . . and Romeo! I know a cat lady who finished a first dinner at hors d'oeuvres when her date told her he detested cats. She stood up and said: 'I'm sure you have many good qualities, but let's not waste each other's time.' That's being clear about what you want! Who is she partnered with now? A man who adores cats as much as she does. What bliss!

Sometimes someone who doesn't like cats will change his mind. But this is far too rare to be counted upon. Cat hating is usually deeply ingrained. According to Pebbles' *Cat Book of Human Psychology*, possible explanations for cat hating include:

♥ Jealousy—He is angered by the thought that you might love your cat more than him. And maybe you do.

- ♥ Illogical Intergenerational Thinking—'My father hated cats, as did his father before him' . . . possibly dating back to the Inquisition.
- ♥ Childhood Trauma—A cat scratched him when he tried to pull its tail.
- ♥ Empathy Deficit Disorder—He cannot understand the appeal of cute, fluffy creatures that purr and bat at sunbeams.
- ♥ Freudian Tendencies—He equates cats with women and is frustrated that he can't control either.
- ♥ Ancestral Memories—He was eaten by a sabre-toothed tiger in a past life.

Better luck next time!

Pebbles 🐾

Cat wisdom

Rocky

'The definition of insanity is chasing your tail. Stop going around in circles. Get a new perspective and go forward.'

✳ ✳ ✳

Friendly vocalisations

Meow ⟶ A greeting usually directed at a human rather than another cat.

A very loud meow ⟶ A command to that same human. Feed me! Wake up! Open the door!

Chirp ⟶ Cats make this rolling meow sound when they are about to receive something they want, such as a meal, some attention, or your lap. A mother cat vocalises like this when she tells her kittens to follow her. Your cat wants you to follow its instructions: 'put the food in the bowl' or 'let me sit on you'.

Trill ➤⎯⎯➤ A very affectionate greeting (sounds like a musical 'Mrrh!').

Murmur ➤⎯⎯➤ Often part of the purring process and suggests a relaxed greeting.

Purring ➤⎯⎯➤ Usually a contented sound, but also a self-soothing sound when a cat is fearful or hurt.

Hostile vocalisations

Stay away from any cat that is making any of the following sounds to you. If it is a frightened cat that you are trying to settle in to your home, use comforting language towards the cat but don't try to touch it or pick it up. Give the cat a box to hide in or a high place to sit. It will eventually calm down.

Chattering ➤⎯⎯➤ Your cat might make a chattering sound when it sees prey but can't reach it; for example, when it sees a bird on the other side of the window glass. It is frustrated that it can't eat it. Some behaviourists suggest the cat is practising its killing bite. One of my cats, Gucci, used to make this sound at a man in my life who turned out to be a very bad person. I can't help thinking that Gucci sensed something was wrong long before I did!

Growl ➤⎯⎯➤ This is a warning. Pay attention to it.

Hiss ➤——→ A sound made by a frightened or threatened cat. It has been suggested cats are imitating the sound of a snake (a cat's mortal enemy) in order to frighten away other cats and possibly you. Remember, a frightened cat is just as likely to attack as an aggressive one, so use comforting language towards the cat or ignore it until it calms down.

Spit ➤——→ This is a sudden, short expulsion of air usually given at the end of a hiss. The sound is emitted to make you jump. And jump you should, just as if a snake was about to strike!

Cat etiquette

Cats have a great sense of dignity and self-respect. Have you ever seen a cat attempt to jump on a shelf and miss its target? Did you notice the cat immediately look around to see if anyone noticed? Never laugh at your cat. Its pride will be severely bruised. As long as your cat hasn't hurt itself, the best thing you can do is pretend you didn't see the mishap.

You may have had the experience of lying on the sofa or reading in bed and your cat has jumped onto your chest and pressed its nose to yours. You patted your cat and then it turned around and showed you its butt? You may have ·--→

thought that the second part of this ritual was a bit rich, but in terms of cat social etiquette your cat is paying you a compliment! When you stroke your cat, it remembers the pleasure it received from its mother's affection. Its mother also used to clean its little butt with her tongue. Don't worry, you don't have go that far!

Can a cat be trained?

Can a cat be trained? The short answer: ABSOLUTELY!

We never question whether dogs can be trained. They are highly social animals and most of us are aware of puppy schools, police dog training academies, airport sniffer dogs and guide-dog charities. Dog owners recognise the need to train their canines. An untrained dog can be a liability, difficult to live with and possibly even dangerous.

Dogs need masters. This makes sense because they are pack animals and are used to following a leader. If you don't like giving orders, preferring cooperation, collaboration and group input, a dog may not be the right companion animal for you. Because cats are so self-sufficient, most cat guardians think that not only do cats not need training, they couldn't be trained even if you tried. Those who have acquired kittens rarely find any need to toilet train them. Even cats from stray-cat colonies seem to instinctively know how to use a litter box.

Unfortunately, because of the common notion that training a cat is a lost cause, we often put up with behaviour that is difficult to live with. Many of us have had the experience of telling our cat to get off the kitchen counter or dining table, only to have our cat repeat the behaviour a minute later. It becomes a battle of wills, where the cat is most often the winner. Sadly, many otherwise good cats are surrendered to pounds and shelters each year because of behavioural issues, but cats are intelligent, sensitive creatures that are more than capable of being trained. You just can't train them the same way you train a dog.

Dogs were domesticated long before cats, and cats have not been bred to serve a particular purpose. Dogs are almost completely dependent on their owners, to the point where they will stay loyal even to someone who abuses them. When I was researching my novel *The Invitation*, I came across the chilling story of Claude Bernard, a French physiologist who used to dissect dogs alive in the late 1800s; he was awarded medals for his 'scientific' work and was even honoured with a public funeral. I cried when I read that the dogs he tortured would lick his hands, begging for mercy. Dogs are loyal, no doubt, but sometimes to their own detriment. Cats are loyal too, but only if you treat them well. Treat a cat badly and it will have no hesitation in leaving you and looking for someone who will treat it better. (That's what I love about them. Many of us could learn a lot about healthy relationship standards by watching our cats!)

Cat wisdom

Shadow

*'There are few problems that can't be
solved by taking a good nap!'*

✳ ✳ ✳

Cats don't need masters, but they do need a good mother. Mother cats go through a process of training their kittens. When the litter are very young, the mother cat will hunt for them and bring back dead prey, but when they are weaning she brings back live prey, which the kittens must learn how to hunt and kill. Although the kittens would still like to cuddle up to her to drink her milk, she deliberately lies on her stomach so they can't reach her teats and ignores their cries, knowing if they don't learn to fend for themselves, they won't survive.

To harness your cat's learning style, you have to think like a mother cat and not a master. I picked this up when I had two sister cats, Gardenia and Lilac, and then three brothers,

Valentino, Versace and Gucci. My cats would follow me around wherever I went during the day. They rose when I rose, they stayed in my writing room when I worked, and if I took a break to play the piano they would come with me. When I went to bed, they would settle down for the night too. They seemed always to be looking to me for their cue about what to do next.

At some level you have already trained your cat. Have you noticed that it suddenly appears in the kitchen when you open the cupboard where the cat food is kept? Or it wanders into your bedroom when it hears your alarm clock go off? Why do you think your cat places itself in front of your computer screen when you are working or sits on your book or newspaper to stop you from reading it? It has learned that such behaviour gets it attention.

Cats love attention. They especially love positive attention, but they will use negative behaviour if that gets attention too. They know that nudging your favourite vase off a table will immediately get you up from whatever you are doing. If you understand that your cat wants attention, you are halfway to learning how to train it: reinforce positive behaviour and ignore bad behaviour (unless the cat is about to jump on a hot stove!)

Punishment will not work with your cat. This is because cats live in the present moment. When you come home and find that your cat has chewed through its dry-food bag and eaten all the contents, scolding it won't work. Your cat doesn't associate your anger with anything it has done. It was naughty an hour ago and this is now. Rather, it thinks there is a problem with you. When it slinks off, that's not guilt: cats make themselves as small and inconspicuous as possible when they are afraid and at that moment when you are scolding your cat, it is afraid of you. Not because it thinks it has done something wrong, but because it is worried you have lost your marbles.

Dogs in the wild live in packs and depend on each other for survival. Cats, however, place more importance on their territory. That's why they sniff and mark it so much. They have to know that everything in their territory is familiar in order to feel secure. That includes you. So if you start behaving erratically, they will feel very unsafe indeed. Do this enough times and your cat will display nervous and stressed behaviour around you.

Cats love activity, they love having their minds and senses stimulated, and they love learning from the people who love them. And it doesn't matter what age your cat is: an old cat can learn new tricks!

....

Stately, kindly, lordly friend,
Condescend
Here to sit by me.
Algernon Charles Swinburne (English poet, 1837–1909)

What can you teach a cat?

♥ To come when you call.

♥ To sit and stay.

♥ To get along with other cats and new people.

♥ To curb aggression (after you have checked that the cause is not health or environment related).

♥ To not jump on kitchen counters.

♥ To not dart at doors.

♥ To not scratch furniture.

♥ To be calm at the veterinary surgery.

♥ To let you give it pills, cut its claws and brush its teeth.

♥ To roll over and high-five with you.

♥ If you have a very active cat, you can teach it to jump through hoops, fetch and even play dead. Just don't expect it to bring you your slippers; that might be a bit below its dignity.

Get your training started with these excellent books

The Trainable Cat, by John Bradshaw and Sarah Ellis
(Penguin Books, 2017)
This book is great for people like me who love to read all the nitty-gritty detail on cat behaviour and want to get inside a cat's head: how they think, how they have evolved, how they view people. It's an extremely thorough book written by two renowned cat behavioural scientists and covers absolutely everything you need to know about cat training. Maybe even a lot more than you would actually need to train your cat. Highly interesting reading.

Naughty No More, by Marilyn Krieger (Lumina Media, 2011)
This is a straightforward book describing the process of clicker training, which is based on the science of operant conditioning. When you are training your cat you use a small device to make a 'click' sound before issuing a reward (such as a small food treat, a pat, a toy) after the cat performs a desired behaviour. Eventually the cat learns that, in order to get that positive attention, it has to get you to make that 'click' sound and to do that it has to perform the desired behaviour again. Not all trainers use a clicker, but advocates of the method claim it is the fastest way to teach a cat to do what you want. I have personally found this to work well. --→

Cat Training in 10 Minutes, by Miriam Fields-Babineau (TFH Publications, 2003)

As the title suggests, this book gets right to the basics of training by positive reinforcement. If you are feeling a little sceptical that you will be able to train your cat, start with this book. Follow its instructions, stick with the program and eventually you will not only surprise yourself with what your cat can learn and do, but you will also be able to amaze your friends.

7

Indoors or outdoors?

I n the last few decades there has been a trend for cats to be kept indoors full-time and this reflects the changing role of the cat from mouser to companion. Indoor cats have much longer life spans than their outdoor counterparts. While an indoor cat may live fifteen to eighteen years, the average life span for an outdoor cat can be as short as two years. Many guardians realise that cats left outdoors face a number of dangers including motor vehicle collisions, aggressive dogs, predation by wild animals, injuries from cat fights and diseases such as feline leukaemia and feline AIDS. There is also the potential heartbreak of an animal that disappears and the fate of which always remains unknown. The other thing to consider is that while you might enjoy having a member

Cat wisdom

Samson

'"Meow!" And the door shall be opened unto you.'

✳ ✳ ✳

of the feline species in your garden, it's not fair to let your cat wander around the garden of a neighbour who may not appreciate it eating their pond fish, burying its waste in the children's sandpit or terrorising the birds that stop to take a drink at the birdbath. I'm sure if your neighbour wandered around your garden behaving the same way, you would be horrified! If you want your cat to spend time outside then it is only courteous to find a way to keep it on your own property. Doing so will also protect your cat from anyone who might want to do it harm (your infuriated neighbour, for instance).

Cat guardians are becoming as vigilant over their animal companions as good parents are over their children. And that's a positive thing for cats. Most cats still live indoor–outdoor lifestyles, but in Australia particularly this poses problems for our wildlife. Even in our cities we are blessed with an abundance of native fauna. Right now, while I am writing this, there is a red-plumed king parrot perched in the tree outside my window, along with his emerald-feathered queen. Throughout the day I will be treated to visits from crimson rosellas, rainbow lorikeets and kookaburras. Dainty fairy wrens will flit in and out of the shrubbery and, when the sun goes down, the garden will come alive with possums carrying their young on their backs. If I go out with a torch to watch them I will catch the reflection of the mirror-like eyes of boobook owls and tawny frogmouths peering down at me from the trees. Most city dwellers around the world only have a chance to enjoy this parade of nature's splendour if they own a country house, but I'm less than half an hour's drive from Sydney's Central Business District. Australian wildlife is unique and precious.

In my volunteer work with a wildlife rescue and rehabilitation organisation, cat attack was the most common reason animals came into care in suburban areas. But just because a volunteer collects an animal that was attacked doesn't mean it will survive. It was heartbreaking to have to pick up all those bleeding, torn and paralysed bodies, knowing all that could be done for them was to have them humanely euthanised as quickly as possible. Even those that did survive the injuries from the attack often died later. If we couldn't get antibiotics into them quickly enough—some say a small window of only a few

hours—the bacteria in a cat's saliva, which native fauna has no resistance to, would kill them. And these are the animals that were actually found. So many more would have died lingering, painful deaths with nobody noticing. The most frustrating thing for me as a rescuer, and a cat lover, was to face the people who were in complete denial about their cat's impact on wildlife. 'Oh no, my Bobby-boy never kills anything. He just watches the birds in the garden and shows no interest.' It would be shocking for them if someone attached a camera to Bobby-boy's collar and they were to witness what he actually got up to, especially if they left him out all night.

Cats are expert hunters; they are patient and silent stalkers, and lightning quick when they want to pounce. In a study that sparked quite a lot of controversy in Australia, David Paton, a zoologist at The University of Adelaide, claimed that even a well-fed outdoor domestic cat* will kill, on average, sixteen mammals, eight birds and eight reptiles a year. Although some argue that the study was somewhat biased in its methods,

---

* *'Domestic cat' refers to cats that have human guardians. To a certain degree, this intersects with stray-cat colonies in the city areas (where the cats eat mainly rats and mice or forage in rubbish bins, unless they are monitored by cat charities employing trap-neuter-return-and-feed programs). I am not referring to true feral cats that have gone wild in bushland and outback areas.*

further research has indicated that domestic cats do indeed impact wildlife negatively. When you consider all the other odds against native birds and animals in suburban areas anyway—motor vehicles, land clearance, garden poisons and so on—outdoor domestic cats can push local wildlife to the tipping point.

Because of that, I encourage others to consider the wildlife around them. Let those animals be free to enjoy their native habitat, while cats stay indoors to enjoy the company and attention of their doting guardians. But for the welfare of our cats, we also need to make sure that we are providing them with stimulating indoor environments.

No scapecats

It's important to also recognise the human impact on wildlife and not blame everything on cats alone. According to the World Wildlife Fund, Australia has one of the worst land-clearance records in the world, and in the past twenty years 7.7 million hectares of threatened-species habitat have been wiped out. The Nature Conservation Council estimates that every day in New South Wales alone, 23 football fields of koala habitat is bulldozed. On the outskirts of our cities, what used to be green belts and wildlife corridors are now filled with housing estates with no gardens or street trees and insubstantially vegetated parkland. Further to that, we have become a throwaway society, and more and more land has become nothing but a receptacle for our wastefulness.

Then there is the issue of how our actions affect climate change. In recent years, the Australian bushfire season has been increasing in length and severity. Millions of animals and fragile ecosystems can—and have—been wiped out in a matter of hours with each burn, and yet Australia's ability to address climate change has been constantly stymied by a posse of climate change-denying politicians. We have lost valuable time because of them.

So everyone needs to look at their actions holistically if we really want to take good care of the planet and all of the creatures on it. Certainly as cat lovers we can make a great impact by being responsible for our animals—having our cats desexed and keeping them happy and entertained indoors—and encouraging friends and family to do the same. Every step is progress and we all have a part to play.

Dear Pebbles,

On social media today I saw a beautiful cat, Tommy, who is up for adoption. I would very much like to give him a home but I'm not sure if my present cat, Darcy, would approve. My friend tried to introduce a new cat to her household and now her once tranquil home is under a blitzkrieg of hissing, spitting and spraying. Is there a right way to go about introducing a new cat to your resident one?
Concerned

Dear Concerned:

I would like you to imagine this: one evening you are sitting there in your living room watching television, when your husband arrives home with a man you've never laid eyes on in your life before. 'Hello darling,' your husband says. 'This is Bob. He's going to be living with us now.'

Now, you don't know the first thing about Bob. Are you just going to say, 'Oh, that's very nice, dear! Hello Bob'? I should think not. I should imagine you would make a great deal of fuss about the situation. There you were all cosy in the privacy of your home and now suddenly there is this Bob fellow everywhere, eating off your plates, sleeping in your bed and sitting on your toilet with the door wide open. Heavens! So why do you expect Darcy might feel any different when you turn up with Tommy? Yes, kittens, like children, make friends easily. We adults are selective. Any cat worth their whiskers expects formality and respect when it comes to introductions. Getting to know someone takes time.

Now I'm going to say this very clearly. When it comes to felines, there is a number-one rule: slow is fast and fast is slow. If you go through the protocol I am about to share with you, slowly and patiently (and it may take anywhere from one week to several to achieve the desired result), you will very likely create a situation where Darcy and Tommy can become lifelong friends who will eat, play and sleep together. But I warn you, Concerned, if you rush this process or skip steps you may well spend the next ten to fifteen years in Kitty Armageddon. Firstly, you will need to settle Tommy into one room in your house where Darcy doesn't have access. Then when he is settled, you can begin a proper feline introduction.

Smell ➺⟶ Before they even lay eyes on each other, Darcy and Tommy need to exchange scents. Get a pair of clean socks. Rub one all over Darcy and give it to Tommy to sniff. Then do the same with Tommy and let Darcy smell the sock. Do this a few times then put the exchange sock in the other cat's bed. After this, let Tommy explore Darcy's areas of the house while Darcy is locked away. Tommy will rub his cheeks on furniture legs and corners to deposit his scent on them. Then let Darcy do the same in Tommy's room while Tommy is put somewhere else. Now you are ready for the touchstone of smell exchange. Take some of Darcy's used litter and put it in Tommy's tray and vice versa for Tommy's litter in Darcy's tray. Only a small amount is needed. Think of it like a dating profile or business card. Tommy and Darcy will be able to get all the information they need about each other this way: their ages, their genders, their dreams for the future and perhaps even their star signs.

Sound ➤⟶ Feed Tommy on one side of the door of his room and Darcy on the other, so they can get to know each other's dinner etiquette. Is Tommy a loud masticator or discreet? Does Darcy wheeze when he swallows? If they play footsies with each other under the door, that is excellent progress. But if they snarl, then this is an indication that you will have to continue a little longer on the exchange of smells and sounds before progressing further.

Sight ➤⟶ Think of it as that moment when the contestants of *Perfect Match* get to see each other for the first time after answering all those tricky get-to-know-you questions: Surprise! Shock! Delight! Dismay! 'Oh my goodness! Am I really going on a seven-day all-expenses-paid holiday to Hawaii with this person?' All those emotions, all at once. For this reason, it's best if the cats view each other with some sort of protective screen between them in the first instance. Some pros do this with a baby barrier gate or screen door, but if you can't remodel your home then you can get away with a cat carrier (as long as you have helped Darcy and Tommy to be comfortable in their cat carriers first by feeding them in them and letting them use the carriers as beds). A synthetic cat pheromone product would be an excellent icebreaker at this stage. Gradually move the cat carriers closer together over successive days for incrementally longer periods of time until Darcy and Tommy seem quite settled in each other's company.

Tada! The day has arrived when you can let Darcy and Tommy freely interact with each other. Remember to give them their own litter boxes and food dishes. Giving them vertical territory such as chairs they can sit on separately if they need to, cat towers, beds on top of cupboards and shelves, and so on, will also help keep things progressing smoothly. Even the closest of cats need their own personal space. Expect some hisses and growls in this period, but if there is outright aggression go back to step one and begin again.

Congratulations on a happy, lifelong pairing!

239

Keeping your cat indoors

The best way to ensure your kitty's longevity, safety and good health is to keep them indoors; however, you need to take a few steps to avoid the tendency of indoor cats to become overweight due to insufficient activity, or to develop behavioural problems from a lack of stimulation. Here's how to keep your indoor cat happy, healthy and entertained.

Private and personal space

An indoor cat is much more likely to interact with its guardian and bond with them. But even the friendliest cat needs some 'alone time'. Make sure that your cat has a cosy place where it can hide away from the world when desired: a bed on top of an accessible cupboard or hidden in a nook is perfect. Even a box with a blanket in it, tucked under a chair or desk, will make a good hideaway. Secluded, private spaces are especially important in multi-cat households and open-plan homes.

Exercise and stimulation

Obesity is a major problem in indoor cat populations and can lead to illnesses such as diabetes, heart disease and cancer. Behavioural issues often arise out of boredom, as they do with children, and even adults for that matter. Here are some ways to get your cat's body moving and its brain stimulated at the same time.

Faux hunting ➤——➤ In the wild, cats hunt for their food and can eat up to twenty small meals a day (and I mean small—the size of a mouse). They are used to roaming and stalking before each catch. They earn their food. Indoor cats usually have their food plonked down in front of them, or worse, left in an overfilled bowl for them to graze on. Constant food should only be available for elderly or sick cats that need to keep their weight up. Otherwise, if your cat is healthy, make it work a little for its food:

- Instead of putting the food down in front of your cat, get it to follow you and chase you around the house a few times. Go from room to room holding the dish of food in front of you. Go up and down the hallway a few times, or even better, up and down stairs if you live in a multilevel house. You only have to do this for a few minutes (your cat's steps are much smaller than yours). If you do this two or three times a day, your cat—and possibly you too—will get fit in no time! Put the food down in different areas each time so that your cat doesn't try to outsmart you by sitting in the one spot while you go round and round. (Another tip from me on this one: remember to watch where you are going! More than once I've walked into a door somebody has closed.)

- Puzzle feeders are another great way to get your cat working for its food. You can buy these from pet-supply stores or you can watch videos online to learn how to make them easily and inexpensively on your own (stock up on empty toilet rolls beforehand).

Toys ⇒—→ Make time to play with your cat. It should be fun for both of you. Cats are creatures of habit, so if you pick a regular time of day to play with your cat, it will look forward to those times with you and your bond will deepen. Several short sessions are better than longer ones.

- Experiment with the toys that work best for your kitty and swap them around on a regular basis, so that it doesn't get bored with one type of toy. The toys that I find work best include plush mice, rubber balls and toys on the end of a pole.

- Toys on the end of a pole are particularly attractive to cats, but I find that the toys on most store-bought poles are too big and scare my cats. I usually replace the toy with a sparkly string of curled ribbon, or a piece of paper crinkled into a bow (this makes a rustling sound that is appealing to cats, and it can easily be replaced as your cat shreds the paper). A good rule for toy size with regard to both appeal and safety is to choose something that your cat or kitten could carry easily in its jaws—say, the size of a mouse rather than as small as a beetle or as large as an adult rat. Too small, and there is a danger of the toy getting caught in the cat's airways; too large, and your cat might feel intimidated. Also be aware of any parts of a toy (eyes and ears on toy mice, for example) that could come off and choke your cat.

A game I have found that works very well with my own cat companions as well as with foster cats is to put a towel on the floor and poke the handle end of a play pole in and out from under it, in the manner of a lizard playing hide and seek. This is a great game if you have a lazy cat or an older one that isn't in the habit of playing. I haven't yet found a cat that can resist this game! The cat usually ends up wrestling the towel and kicking it with its back legs, which is also great exercise.

- Laser toys can be fun, but end the game by shining the beam on a toy mouse so your cat feels like it has actually caught something (otherwise your cat can become frustrated at its lack of hunting accomplishment). Never shine the laser directly into your cat's eyes (or let young children play with it unsupervised).

- If you are away for most of the day, you can fold
  a towel on the floor and place some toys on it for
  your cat. Soft toy mice and ping-pong balls are good
  choices. There is something about a towel on the
  floor that is irresistible to cats and you may find that
  your cat wrestles with it as well as playing with the
  toys. Put the toys away when you come home, so that
  your cat sees them as something deliciously secret
  to get up to when you are away. As the saying goes,
  'When their human is away, the cats will play' . . . or
  something like that!

Climbing ➻⟶ Most cats love to climb, so give your cat
furniture that it is allowed to clamber over. Cat towers,
scratching posts and wall-mounted platforms can all
serve this purpose.

- Towers are best placed near (closed) windows so your
  cat can view the world outside.

- Provide both vertical and horizontal scratching posts.
  Vertical posts should be tall and steady so your cat
  can have a good stretch. Sisal rope is the surface
  cats like best for scratching (other than your most
  expensive furniture, of course).

- If you have a street view or a garden outlook, make sure there is space on the windowsill for your cat to spend time there watching the activity outside. If you face an uninspiring view such as a brick wall you can spice it up with some attractive hanging plants on the outside of the glass (flowers will attract bees and other insects), or soft-sound wind chimes or a bird mobile that flutters in the breeze.

Water fountain ⊶⟶ Most cats don't drink enough, and running water is often more appealing to cats than still water so a drinking fountain can encourage your cat to drink more water as well as provide some interest for it. Fountains come in all shapes and sizes, and some make beautiful home decor, but the most important feature is that they should be easy to clean. I find ones that I can put in the dishwasher the most convenient to clean regularly.

Outdoor cat enclosures and tunnels ⊶⟶ Enclosures and tunnels are a practical way for your cat to get fresh air and sunshine, as well as having the stimulation of watching garden activity without harming wildlife. If you plan to leave your cat in an enclosure while you are away from home, make sure that it has adequate shelter from rain, storms and hot sunshine. Provide plenty of drinking water. Don't leave your cat in an outdoor enclosure during heatwaves: heat stroke can kill a cat quickly.

Walking leads ⚬⟶ Some cats take to these and just prance along, but most cats will simply wander and sniff flowers and plants, so see this more as a stimulation activity rather than exercise for fitness. I used to walk one of my cats in the garden with the lead in one hand and a cup of tea in the other: this will give you an idea of the pace you can expect! When I lived in New York, I would often see a man walking his Siamese cat along Fifth Avenue on a lead, but personally I've never taken my cats further than my garden fence—I'm too wary of what might happen if we encounter a vicious dog or the cat gets a sudden scare and runs off and gets lost.

- Be aware that if you take your indoor cat outside, even occasionally, you will need to give it flea and tick protection. If other cats wander into your garden, then your indoor cat will also need to be vaccinated.

- Train your cat to walk on the lead inside your house first before you take it outside. Get your cat used to wearing the harness for a few days, then attach the lead and practise with that inside. When you go outdoors, stay close to your entry door for the first few days before going further afield in the garden.

You

According to Dr John Bradshaw, founder of the Anthrozoology Institute in the United Kingdom and a Visiting Fellow in Anthrozoology at the University of Bristol*, cats view us differently to the way dogs do. Dogs see us as a separate species and change their behaviour depending on whether they are dealing with a human or a fellow dog. Cats, on the other hand, view us as other cats (albeit slightly clumsier and less elegant ones). In fact, I would go so far as to suggest that cats generally view their guardians as their mother cats. They love the care we lavish on them, so the best way to keep your cat stimulated is to enjoy interacting with it. Brush your cat if they enjoy that, talk to them softly, sing to them if you like. Practise your foreign languages with your cat or read your poetry out loud to it. Although your cat won't understand a word of what you are saying, you will find it an appreciative audience. Cats love routines and they enjoy watching you go through yours. Ever wonder why your cat bursts through the door when you go to the bathroom? Your cat is fascinated by you: it wants to know what you are doing behind that door!

---

* Anthrozoology is the science of human–animal interactions, including the study of the behaviour and welfare of domestic cats and dogs, and their relationships with people.

Transitioning from outdoors to indoors

If you have—or have inherited—a cat that has lived outdoors and you would like it to live indoors, the key to this transition is to do it gradually.

If the cat is already familiar with you and your home:

- ♥ Winter is the best time to transition an outdoor cat into living indoors. Cats love warmth and a snuggly warm bed by a heater is a great enticement to stay indoors.

- ♥ If your cat isn't desexed, get it desexed. It will be near impossible to keep an undesexed cat happily indoors.

- ♥ Start feeding your cat indoors. If they are nervous about coming inside, put the food dishes just inside an open doorway and gradually move the dishes further and further inside as the cat gains more confidence.

- ♥ If they have never used a litter tray before, train your cat to use one before you move them indoors. You can leave the litter tray in a spot in the garden they frequent or on your back balcony if the cat spends time there. Cats like to dig into soft material, so the litter tray will be attractive to them.

♥ Gradually encourage your cat to spend more time indoors. You could keep it inside after its last meal for the day and let it out first thing in the morning, then progressively increase the amount of time spent indoors.

♥ If you want your cat to be indoors full time, you will need to make the interior of your house as stimulating to it as the outside world, by following the advice I've already given. When your cat goes to an exterior door and meows to go out, entice it into another activity, either by playing a game or offering a cat treat in order to persuade it to stay with you on the sofa.

♥ If you want to keep a cat in transition indoors when you go out, give it a designated room to stay in with a comfy bed and other enticing treats. If the room is carpeted, you might want to place a thin piece of plywood on the floor at the door so your cat doesn't scratch the carpet there in an attempt to get out.

♥ If you are transitioning more than one cat, give them plenty of vertical territory (cat towers, beds on top of cupboards, wall-mounted platforms, and so on). Although the cats may have been friends outside the home, they will renegotiate territories once inside. Give them their own litter trays and dishes.

If the cat is unfamiliar with you and your home:

♥ Treat the cat as you would any new cat you were bringing into your house. Give it a designated room with hideaway spaces, food and water dishes and a litter tray.

♥ Spend time with the cat and let it get comfortable with both you and the room before you let the cat explore further afield in the house.

♥ Synthetic cat pheromones can be used to help to calm an unsettled cat.

♥ Once the cat is used to you and the interior of the house, give it a good reason to remain inside by ensuring that it stays happy, healthy and entertained.

♥ Make sure the cat is microchipped with your up-to-date details. While inside you could train the cat to wear an elasticised collar with your mobile phone number on a tag attached to it. This way, if the cat escapes, you have a much better chance that it will be returned to you when found.

....

He walked by himself, and all places were alike to him.
Rudyard Kipling (English author, 1865–1936)
from 'The Cat that Walked by Himself'

As our cats increasingly become much-loved members of our families rather than mere pest controllers, it's natural that we want to take the best care of them. Because indoor cats live much longer lives than their outdoor counterparts, more and more guardians are choosing to keep their cats inside, at least most of the time. This is not only a good situation for cats but also for local wildlife populations that are already suffering challenges due to human encroachment on their habitat. Adding predation by domestic cats to the mix could drive many of these vulnerable species to extinction; however, cats have active minds and physical needs, so it's important to keep them stimulated and active. The best way to do this is to provide them with enticing indoor activities and environments, as well as with your loving company.

8

The end of the tale

I hope that *The Divine Feline: A chic cat lady's guide to woman's best friend* has given you as much joy to read as it gave me to write!

Understanding that there is a long association between the feline and the feminine, and the possibility of a profound spiritual connection with our cat companions, gives us an ability to more deeply appreciate them, ourselves and the sacredness of life.

I encourage you to continue to learn as much as you can about your feline friend's behaviour and physiology. The deeper and more fully we understand and appreciate something we love, the more joy and passion it infuses into the relationship. Happy cats make happy guardians and vice versa!

There is also much we can learn from our cats, including making better use of our senses—smell, sound, touch, taste and sight—in order to fine-tune our awareness and therefore our appreciation of the world around us. This keeps us firmly anchored in the present moment, which is pretty much where a cat's mind rests. Developing our five basic senses also leads to that special sixth sense that both cats and women are known to especially possess: the ability to perceive the mysterious, unseen aspects of life.

I heartily urge you to adopt your cat's self-esteem and independence; to remember that you are beautiful just as you are; and to never stay with anybody who treats you badly. You can survive on your own if need be, but most likely there are plenty of other kinder people who would be happy to have you around.

Don't let anyone belittle you or discourage you because you love cats. I was surprised to learn that some people don't post pictures of their cats on social media as much as they would love to, because they are worried that they might be perceived as freaky loners. Obviously, I did not get the memo on that one! But even if I did, I wouldn't have cared less. Is loving cats so much more odd than liking racing cars, shouting at football matches or playing chess? There is nothing wrong with those interests and there is nothing wrong with yours. The feminine and the feline have been belittled enough. It's time to take our power back.

So, my chic cat ladies, prance boldly into your fabulous feline-loving futures with a swish of your majestic tail and a mysterious glint in your alluring eyes!

Acknowledgements

My acknowledgements page for *The Divine Feline: A chic cat lady's guide to woman's best friend* feels like a gratitude list, so I'm going to write it as one. I am so grateful for:

♥ My beautiful publisher, Kelly Doust, at Murdoch Books, who first suggested the idea of writing a cat book to me, thus providing me with hours of fun that I could pass off as 'real work'.

♥ The wonderful team at Murdoch Books and also my fabulous editors Julie Mazur Tribe and Melody Lord.

♥ My agent, Catherine Drayton, who is so good with the practical side of producing books.

♥ Neryl Walker, who provided the gorgeous illustrations, and Madeleine Kane, who created the design, that made the book a pleasure to behold.

♥ Halina Thompson and the tireless volunteers at the World League for Protection of Animals, Australia, whose compassion for animals is both heartwarming and inspiring.

♥ My friends and family who always support me.

♥ My beautiful cats, both past and present, who have brought so much joy into my life (Snuggy, Fluffy, Gardenia and Lilac, and Valentino, Versace and Gucci) as well as all the precious rescue cats I have had the pleasure of crossing paths with.

And finally, I'm grateful for all of my fellow cat ladies. Although we may have never met, I feel that we have so much in common, especially with regard to our love for a magnificient animal that embodies so many of our mysterious feminine attributes and connects us with the Divine.

With purrs and cuddles,

Belinda Alexandra

Belinda Alexandra

Belinda Alexandra is the author of nine bestselling novels and has been published around the world including the United States, Spain, France, Germany, the United Kingdom, Turkey, Hungary and Poland. She is the daughter of a Russian mother and an Australian father and has been an intrepid traveller since her youth.

Belinda currently lives in Sydney with her three black cats, Valentino, Versace and Gucci. When she is not catering to their every need, she enjoys flamenco and belly dancing, playing the piano and attempting to wrap her tongue around foreign languages. Belinda is the patron of the World League for Protection of Animals, Australia.

Facebook.com/BelindaAlexandraAuthor/
instagram.com/belinda_alexandra_author

Notes

Chapter 1

9   *Classical Cats: The rise and fall of the sacred cat*, by Donald W. Engels
     (Routledge, 1999)

15   Quoted in *Women & Cats: The history of a love affair*, compiled by
     Michelle Lovric (Chicago Review Press, 2003)

38   'angry but quite unharmed' *Ark Royal: The life of an aircraft carrier at
     war 1939–41*, by William Jameson (Periscope Publishing, 2004)

41   'We shouldn't have done it' Wikipedia contributors, 'Oleg Gazenko',
     Wikipedia, The Free Encyclopedia, https://en.wikipedia.org/w/index.
     php?title=Oleg_Gazenko&oldid=932906039 (accessed 8 April 2020).

41   Quoted in *Cat*, by Katharine M. Rogers (Reaction Books, 2006)

44   *guinnessworldrecords.com*: www.guinnessworldrecords.com/
     news/2017/3video-meet-maru-mugumogu--the-cardboard-box-loving-
     record-breaking-cat (accessed 8 April 2020)

44   *guinnessworldrecords.com*: www.guinnessworldrecords.com/
     world-records/444693-most-views-for-an-animal-on-youtube
     (accessed 8 April 2020)

44   *guinnessworldrecords.com*: www.guinnessworldrecords.com/
     world-records/465511-most-followers-for-a-cat-on-instagram
     (accessed 8 April 2020)

NOTES

47   J. Holt-Lunstad, T.B. Smith, J.B. Layton, 'Social Relationships and Mortality
      Risk: A meta-analytic review', *PLoS Med* 7(7): e1000316 (2010).
      https://doi.org/10.1371/journal.pmed.1000316

Chapter 2
54   *Concerning Cats*, by Helen M. Winslow (Lothrop Publishing Co, 1900)

57   *The Greedy Cat*, Fable iii

72   'Les natures délicates comprennent le chat. Il a pour lui les femmes; en
      grande estime le tiennent les poëtes & les artistes, mus par un système
      nerveux d'une exquise délicatesse, & seules les natures grossières
      méconnaissent la nature distinguée de l'animal.' *Les Chats*, by
      Champfleury, (J. Rothschild, 1869)

73   *The Honeymoon Effect*, by Bruce H. Lipton (Hay House UK Ltd, 2014)

83   *The Doctor, &c.*, Vol IV, by Robert Southey (Lingman, Rees, Orme, Brown,
      Green and Longman, 1837)

90   'Kira jumped from my stomach' *Wild Lavender*, by Belinda Alexandra
      (HarperCollins, 2005)

102   *The Belgian Essays: Charlotte and Emily Brontë*, edited and translated
      by Sue Lonoff (Yale University Press, 1996)

113   *The Proverbs and Epigrams of John Heywood (A.D. 1562)*, (Spenser
      Society, 1867)

117   'Lily frowned. "I don't understand' *Sapphire Skies*, by Belinda Alexandra
      (HarperCollins, 2015)

134   from notebook, 1894; *Kansas City Star*, 5 April 1905. Reported in:
      www.thegreatcat.org/cats-19th-century-part-13-mark-twains-cats/
      (accessed 6 April 2020)

Chapter 4
170   Reported in: www.pbs.org/tesla/ll/story_youth.html (accessed
      6 April 2020)

176   'Why do cats purr?', by Leslie A Lyons, *Scientific American*, 3 April 2006
      (Springer Nature America, Inc)

176 *Essais* Bk. 2, Ch. 2 (1580, ed. M. Rat, 1958)

177 A.I. Qureshi, M.Z. Memon, G. Vazquez and M.F. Suri, 'Cat ownership and the Risk of Fatal Cardiovascular Diseases. Results from the Second National Health and Nutrition Examination Study Mortality Follow-up Study'. *Journal of vascular and interventional neurology*, 2(1), 132–135 (2009). www.ncbi.nlm.nih.gov/pmc/articles/PMC3317329/ (accessed 8 April 2020)

Chapter 5

187 'Can classical music calm your cat?' by Richard Gray, *Daily Mail Online*, 31 March 2015. www.dailymail.co.uk/sciencetech/article-3018343/ Can-classical-music-calm-cat-Playing-violin-relaxes-felines-AC-DC-make-stressed-study-reveals.html (accessed 8 April 2020)

187 'Adagio for Strings', by Samuel Barber, *String Quartet*, Op. 11. 1936

187 *Orchestral Suite No. 3 in D major*, second movement, by Johann Sebastian Bach, BWV 1068.

198 Collected by John Ray (1627–1705) in *English Proverbs* (no. 109)

Chapter 6

225 'To a Cat', *The Poems of Algernon Charles Swinburne*, 6 vols, (Chatto & Windus, 1894)

Chapter 7

233 'Should the cat take the rap?', by Ian Anderson, *New Scientist*, Issue 1926, 21 May 1994.

233 'Feral and pet cats are hunting and killing billions of animals each year in Australia', by Gary-Jon Lysaght and Nick Kilvert, *ABC News*, 15 July 2019. www.abc.net.au/news/2019-07-15/cats-kill-billions-of-animals-each-year-in-australia/11307684 (accessed 8 April 2020)

234 'How Australia became one of the worst deforesters in the world', *Triple J Hack*, 31 October 2018. www.abc.net.au/triplej/programs/hack/how-australia-became-one-of-the-worst-deforesters-in-the-world/10452336 (accessed 8 April 2020)

234 'Australia cleared 7.7 million hectares of threatened species habitat since introduction of environment act' by Lisa Cox, *The Guardian*, 9 September 2019. www.theguardian.com/environment/2019/sep/09/australia-cleared-77m-hectares-of-threatened-species-habitat-since-introduction-of-environment-act (accessed 8 April 2020)

235 'A parliamentary inquiry on the NSW koala population' www.nature.org.au/blog/2019/07/the-nsw-koala-inquiry/ (accessed 8 April 2020)

235 'Have more than a billion animals perished nationwide this bushfire season?', RMIT ABC Fact Check, *ABC News*, 4 February 2020. www.abc.net.au/news/2020-01-31/fact-check-have-bushfires-killed-more-than-a-billion-animals/11912538 (accessed 8 April 2020)

250 'The Cat that Walked by Himself' in *Just So Stories*, by Rudyard Kipling (Doubleday Page, 1912)

About the World League for the Protection of Animals

The World League for Protection of Animals (WLPA) is a 'no-kill' Australian campaign and rescue organisation in Sydney, Australia, which has been fighting for the rights of animals, both native and non-native, since 1935. It runs a cat adoption centre from its head office. It is entirely self-funded through donations and bequests and relies on volunteers.

Facebook.com/wlpaaustralia

wlpa.org

Bibliography

Cat vs. Cat: Keeping peace when you have more than one cat, by Pam Johnson-Bennett (Penguin Books, 2004)

Classical Cats: The rise and fall of the sacred cat, by Donald W. Engels (Routledge, 1999)

Famous Felines: Cats' lives in fact and fiction, by David Alderton (Pen & Sword Books, 2009)

Natural Health Bible for Dogs & Cats: Your A–Z guide to over 200 conditions, herbs, vitamins, and supplements, by Shawn Messonnier (Three Rivers Press, 2001)

Revered and Reviled: A complete history of the domestic cat, by Laura A. Vocelle (Great Cat Publications, 2016)

Sekhmet & Bastet: The feline powers of Egypt, by Lesley Jackson (Avalonia, 2018)

Starting from Scratch: How to correct behavior problems in your adult cat, by Pam Johnson-Bennett (Penguin Books, 2004)

The Cat in Ancient Egypt, by Jaromir Malek (University of Pennsylvania Press, 1997)

When Cats Reigned Like Kings: On the trail of the sacred cats, by Georgie Anne Geyer (Transaction Publishers, 2012)

Why Does My Cat Do That? Answers to the 50 questions cat lovers ask, by Catherine Davidson (Ivy Press, 2008)

Index

INDEX

INDEX